INHALT

KMK-Niveaustufe I
(Europäischer Referenzrahmen A 2 Waystage)

KMK-Niveaustufe II
(Europäischer Referenzrahmen B 1 Threshold)

KMK-Niveaustufe III
(Europäischer Referenzrahmen B 2 Vantage)

REZEPTION HÖRVERSTEHEN
Einsatz der beiliegenden Audio-CD

Listening

Man braucht nicht jedes einzelne Wort zu verstehen, um den Inhalt eines Textes aufzunehmen. Einige Strategien können beim Hörverstehen helfen:

Vor dem Hören:

- Stellen Sie sich vor, in welcher Situation, in welchem thematischen Zusammenhang der Hörtext (z. B. eine Rede, ein Bericht) angesiedelt ist, oder, wenn der Hörtext ein Dialog ist, wer mit wem worüber sprechen könnte.
- Denken Sie an die Vokabeln und Redewendungen, die zu dem Thema des Hörtextes passen könnten.
- Denken Sie daran, welche Art von Sätzen zu dem Hörtext passen könnten, z. B. Fragen, Ausrufe, Gefühlsäußerungen (Gespräch, Interview), sachliche Aussagesätze (Bericht).
- Versuchen Sie vorauszusagen, wie das Thema des Hörtextes lauten könnte.

Während des Hörens:

- Hören Sie sich die Texte von der CD immer zweimal an (in der Prüfung werden die Hörverstehenstexte auch zweimal abgespielt). Machen Sie sich beim ersten Mal immer Notizen. Beim zweiten Hören ergänzen Sie die Notizen und verstehen so immer mehr.
- Sie können Ihre Notizen auch unter bestimmten Aspekten/Überschriften, die Sie beim ersten Hören mitbekommen, ordnen.
- Wenn Sie einen Dialog hören, können Sie z. B. die Namen der Gesprächsteilnehmer in eine Übersicht schreiben und Ihre Notizen in die entsprechenden Abteilungen eintragen.

Außerhalb der Prüfung:

- Wenn Sie einen Film oder eine DVD sehen, können die Bilder Ihnen helfen. Der Hintergrund, die Umgebung, die Sprecher sowie deren Mimik und Gestik unterstützen Sie beim Verstehen.
- Wenn Sie mit jemandem sprechen und Sie verstehen etwas nicht, fragen Sie nach (z. B. *Could you please explain what ... means?*).

Nach dem Hören:

- Gehen Sie Ihre Notizen durch und versuchen Sie, das eine oder andere Detail zu ergänzen. Auf jeden Fall sollten Sie versuchen, aus den Notizen sinnvolle Aussagen zu machen, mündlich oder schriftlich. Dabei fällt Ihnen sicherlich auch noch manches Gehörte wieder ein.

Reading

Beim Lesen von englischen Texten müssen Sie nicht unbedingt jedes Wort verstehen. Machen Sie sich, wenn Sie auf einen unbekannten Text treffen, die folgenden Strategien zunutze:

Vor dem Lesen:

- Machen Sie sich klar, warum Sie den Text lesen werden: Was ist Ihr Leseziel? Zum Beispiel erhoffen Sie sich, bestimmte Informationen zu einem Thema darin zu finden, oder Sie wollen Ihr Wissen über das Thema mit den Informationen und Ideen des Textes vergleichen. Vielleicht möchten Sie auch eine Antwort auf den Text (z. B. einen Brief) oder eine Zusammenfassung schreiben.
- Schauen Sie sich gegebenenfalls die Überschrift an und schreiben Sie die Ideen auf, die Ihnen dazu in den Sinn kommen.
- Eventuell ist der Text illustriert oder enthält eine Tabelle oder Grafik, die Einblick in den Inhalt geben. Versuchen Sie, Anteile des Inhalts „vorauszusehen".

Während des Lesens:

- Lesen Sie den Text einmal ganz durch und versuchen Sie, Ihre vorausgesagten Gedanken mit denen des Textes zu vergleichen. Was ist gleich? Was ist ganz anders in Bezug auf das Thema?
- Fangen Sie nicht an, an dieser Stelle Vokabeln nachzuschlagen. Entdecken Sie erst alles, was Sie verstehen!
- Wenn möglich (z. B. Kopie des Textes o. Ä.), unterstreichen Sie jetzt alles, was Sie verstehen.
- Während der Prüfung zum KMK-Fremdsprachenzertifikat dürfen Sie ein zweisprachiges allgemeines Wörterbuch benutzen. Schlagen Sie daher die Ihnen unbekannten Vokabeln in einem Wörterbuch nach.
- Allerdings sollten Sie nicht jedes unbekannte Wort nachschlagen, sondern sich erst einmal bewusst machen, wovon der Text handelt. Wenn dann wichtige Worte oder Ausdrücke, die für die Lösung benötigt werden, unbekannt sind, ergibt das Nachschlagen im Wörterbuch einen Sinn.

Tipps für die Prüfung:

- Die Arbeitsanweisung kann in englischer oder deutscher Sprache erfolgen. Bevor Sie sich zu sehr um Details kümmern und viel Zeit damit verlieren, einzelne unbekannte – eventuell gar nicht entscheidende Wörter – nachzuschlagen, verschaffen Sie sich erst einmal einen Überblick über die Aufgabe:
    - Welche Art von Text liegt hier vor?
    - Worum geht es grundsätzlich?
- Aufgabentypen, die vorkommen können, sind z. B. Fragen zum Text beantworten, ein Formular oder eine Tabelle ausfüllen, das Beschriften von grafischen Darstellungen, Begriffe oder einzelne Aussagen müssen einem Text oder einer anderen Darstellung zugeordnet werden, Multiple-Choice-Fragen, True/False, die Wiedergabe wichtiger Informationen aus dem Text.

Writing

Wenn Sie einen Text schreiben, gehen Sie am besten Schritt für Schritt vor.
Überlegen Sie zunächst:
Welche Art von Text möchte ich schreiben? Zum Beispiel eine Zusammenfassung, einen Brief oder eine E-Mail? Für jede Textsorte sind ganz bestimmte Dinge wichtig.

In den folgenden kurzen Anleitungen erfahren Sie, wie Sie auf Englisch bestimmte Schreibaufgaben lösen können.

Eine Zusammenfassung (summary) schreiben
Eine Zusammenfassung verkürzt längere Texte. Texte werden zusammengefasst, um einem Leser möglichst knapp und klar den wesentlichen Inhalt zu vermitteln.

- Lesen Sie den ganzen Text einmal oder mehrmals durch, um sich einen Überblick zu verschaffen: Worum geht es? Können Sie wichtige von unwichtigen Informationen unterscheiden? Wenn möglich (z. B. Kopie des Textes o. Ä.), markieren Sie die Stellen, die Sie für unverzichtbar halten.
- Schlagen Sie Vokabeln, deren Bedeutung Ihnen unklar ist, nach.
  Tipp: Wörtliche Rede gehört nicht in eine Zusammenfassung. Wenn der Inhalt der wörtlichen Rede wesentlich ist, schreiben Sie den Text um.
- Lesen Sie Ihre Zusammenfassung und versuchen Sie dabei, die Position des Lesers einzunehmen.

Einen Artikel schreiben
Ein Artikel soll über ein bestimmtes Thema informieren. Er könnte in einer Zeitung, einer Zeitschrift, in einem Buch usw. stehen. Der Verfasser kann zwar seine persönliche Meinung mit in den Artikel aufnehmen, das Hauptziel ist es aber, den Leser oder die Leserin zu informieren, nicht zu überzeugen.

- Überlegen Sie sich eine Überschrift, die deutlich macht, worum es geht.
- Sammeln Sie zunächst alle Ideen, die Sie zu dem Thema haben (in Stichpunkten).
- Finden Sie eine gute Reihenfolge für Ihre Ideen.
- Wählen Sie einige Beispiele aus und beschreiben Sie sie jeweils in einem eigenen Abschnitt näher.
- Beschreiben Sie Ursachen für das Problem.
- Machen Sie Lösungsvorschläge für das Problem.
- Überprüfen Sie, ob die Überschrift noch angebracht ist. Falls nicht, finden Sie eine bessere.

Einen Brief schreiben
Die Form eines Briefes hängt davon ab, an wen Sie schreiben. Ein Brief an eine Freundin/einen Freund sieht anders aus als ein Brief an einen Geschäftspartner oder an eine Behörde: Man spricht von informellen und formellen Briefen.
Grundsätzliches:

- Der Absender gehört in die rechte obere Ecke des Briefbogens.
- Das Datum folgt unter der Adresse des Empfängers auf der linken Seite. Folgende Schreibweisen sind zulässig:
  12/6/09 (US: 6/12/09); 12 June 2009; June 12, 2009; 12th June 2009; June 12th, 2009.
- Anreden:

Ein Mann, Name unbekannt:	Dear Sir
Eine Frau, Name unbekannt:	Dear Madam
Keine Information:	Dear Sir or Madam
Brief an eine Firma:	Dear Sirs
Name bekannt:	Dear Ms Fitzgerald
	Dear Annabelle

- Die erste Zeile des eigentlichen Briefs beginnt mit einem Großbuchstaben.
- Briefe, die mit „Dear Sir“ oder „Dear Madam“ begonnen wurden, enden mit „Yours faithfully“.
- War der Name bekannt, endet ein formeller Brief so: „Yours sincerely“.
- In formellen Briefen vermeidet man Kurzformen wie *don't, he's* usw.

Einen Lebenslauf und eine Bewerbung schreiben

1. Der Lebenslauf

Ein Lebenslauf (CV in Großbritannien, Résumé in den USA) wird erwartet, wenn man sich um einen Job bewirbt, ein Stipendium beantragen will, ein Praktikum machen möchte usw. Der Lebenslauf soll in übersichtlicher Form darstellen, welche Fähigkeiten, Ausbildung und Arbeitserfahrung der Bewerber oder die Bewerberin vorzuweisen hat.

Grundsätzliches:
Zum englischen CV gehören die folgenden Punkte:

- vollständiger Name
- Adresse
- Schulbesuch (mit Daten)
- Arbeitsverhältnisse (mit Daten, Namen und Adressen der Arbeitgeber)
- Ausbildungsgänge und Praktika
- Qualifikationen wie Schulabschluss, Erste-Hilfe-Kurs, Führerschein
- besondere Aufgaben, die Sie schon ausgeführt haben
- besondere Fähigkeiten und Fertigkeiten
- Sprachkenntnisse
- Hobbys und Interessen
- evtl. Namen und Adressen von Personen, die über Sie Auskunft geben können

2. Die Bewerbung

Schreiben Sie einen Brief, in dem Sie klarstellen, für welche Stelle Sie sich bewerben, ab wann Sie die Stelle antreten können und warum Sie sich für die Stelle interessieren. Führen Sie außerdem aus, warum Sie für die Stelle qualifiziert sind.
Fügen Sie Ihren Lebenslauf der Bewerbung bei.

Tipps für die Prüfung:

- Die Arbeitsanweisung kann in englischer oder deutscher Sprache erfolgen.
- Formate, die vorkommen können, sind z. B. E-Mail, Fax, Memo, Brief, Beschreibung eines Produkts/eines Arbeitsablaufs/einer Tätigkeit, Bericht, Fragebogen, Prospekte, Bewerbungsschreiben, Stellenanzeigen, grafische Informationen verbalisieren, Gesprächsnotizen.

Mediation

Mediation bedeutet im Wesentlichen die Übertragung von einer Sprache in die andere.
Dabei geht es eigentlich nicht darum, Wort für Wort zu übersetzen. Eher sollten Sie versuchen, den Sinn einer Aussage oder bestimmte Informationen wiederzugeben.
Sie sollten versuchen, wichtige Wörter zu umschreiben, wenn Ihnen die direkte Übersetzung nicht einfällt.
Wenn Sie vom Deutschen ins Englische übertragen, versuchen Sie, kurze Sätze zu benutzen.

Tipps für die Prüfung:

- Je nach Aufgabenstellung müssen Sie vom Englischen ins Deutsche oder vom Deutschen ins Englische übertragen.
- Bei diesem Aufgabentyp müssen Sie gut auf die Aufgabenstellung achten. Was wird verlangt:
  - genaue Übersetzung
  - sinngemäße Wiedergabe des Inhalts
  - wichtigste Aussagen zusammenfassen
- Achten Sie auch auf Ausdruck und Stil des Textes. Versuchen Sie, den Stil und die Art der Anrede in der Übertragung wiederzugeben.
- Bei der Bewertung der *Mediations*-Aufgaben werden auch der Stil, die Ausdrucksweise und der Inhalt bewertet. Versuchen Sie also, keine wichtigen Sätze oder Aspekte auszulassen.

Lesen Sie regelmäßig Texte aus Büchern, Zeitschriften und Zeitungen, im Internet – das trainiert Ihr Textverständnis und erhöht Ihren Wortschatz. Außerdem erweitern Sie so auch das grundsätzliche Sprachgefühl, das wird Ihnen nicht nur bei den *Mediations*-Aufgaben helfen.

Talking

Hier einige Tipps, die dabei helfen, sich auf Englisch zu unterhalten.
Bevor Sie ein Gespräch beginnen, überlegen Sie sich im Voraus:

- Wie ist die Situation? Geht es z. B. um den Aufbau von Geschäftsbeziehungen oder um Kundenkontakt?
- Was möchten Sie sagen?
- Achten Sie beim Reden auf den Gesichtsausdruck und die Bewegungen Ihres Gesprächspartners.
- Der Tonfall gibt Ihnen Hinweise auf das, was Ihr Gesprächspartner/Ihre Gesprächspartnerin sagt. Am Tonfall können Sie erkennen, ob jemand gerade z. B. verärgert oder zufrieden ist, ungeduldig oder ruhig.
- Wenn Ihnen ein Wort nicht einfällt, umschreiben Sie es. Sie können auch Ihre Hände zu Hilfe nehmen.
- Machen Sie zustimmende Geräusche oder Bewegungen, nicken oder lächeln Sie aufmunternd, um das Gespräch in Gang zu halten.
- Versuchen Sie immer, deutlich zu sprechen.

Tipps für die Prüfung:
Während des mündlichen Teils der Prüfung können natürlich viele verschiedene Themen angesprochen werden.
In den meisten Prüfungen gibt es ein *Warm-up*. Das bedeutet, dass die Prüfung nicht direkt mit der eigentlichen Aufgabe beginnt, sondern erst einmal versucht wird, ins Gespräch zu kommen.

Sobald die Prüfungssituation begonnen hat, kann es sein, dass Sie Aussagen auf Englisch hören und gegebenenfalls darauf reagieren müssen, z. B.

- die Begrüßung
- Fragen nach der Anreise zur Prüfung, Parkplatzsituation
- generelle Aussagen (z. B. über das Wetter, das allgemeine Befinden usw.)
- Anweisungen erfolgen wahrscheinlich auch auf Englisch, z. B.:
  - Please take a seat./Please sit down over there.
  - Can you tell me your name(s)?

Sie sollten darauf vorbereitet sein, etwas über sich selbst zu erzählen, z. B. über Ihre Hobbys oder Ihren Wohnort.
Sie werden aber wahrscheinlich vor allem nach beruflichen Themen gefragt. Bereiten Sie sich also darauf vor, etwas über Ihre Ausbildung im Betrieb zu erzählen oder über Ihren Schulbesuch.
Sie sollten sich auch auf weitergehende Themen wie z. B. Zukunftspläne vorbereiten.
Beispielfragen:

- Can you please tell us something about your company?
- What is a typical work day like?
- What do you like/dislike about your job?

Mündliche Prüfungen können mit einer kurzen Einlesezeit oder einer Vorbereitungszeit beginnen – je nach Aufgabenstellung. Erkundigen Sie sich, was in Ihrem Bundesland üblich ist.

Am besten bereiten Sie sich auf die mündliche Prüfung vor, indem Sie so oft wie möglich Englisch sprechen.

- Stellen Sie sich wichtige Vokabeln und Redewendungen zusammen und lernen Sie diese.
- Es ist auch sehr gut, wenn man häufiger mit einem Partner oder einer Partnerin eine Gesprächssituation probiert.
- Während der Prüfung steht der kommunikative Aspekt im Vordergrund. Fehler werden natürlich registriert und bewertet, aber Hauptsache ist es, mit dem Gegenüber erfolgreich zu kommunizieren.
- Keine Angst vor Fehlern im Ausdruck und in der Grammatik! Wichtig ist, dass der Partner oder die Partnerin versteht, was Sie von ihm/ihr wollen.

1. Taking a message

Susanne Müller arbeitet in der Verkaufsabteilung eines Bürobedarfsgroßhändlers. Sie nimmt einen Anruf für ihre Kollegin entgegen.

Füllen Sie die Telefonnotiz aus.

TELEFONNOTIZ

Anruf angenommen von: ____________________

____

Anruf für: ____________________

Anrufer (Name und Firma): __________ **Telefonnummer:** __________

Referenznummer: ____________________

Grund des Anrufs: ____________________

2. Rooms available

Arne Weiher möchte für eine Messe in Edinburgh mehrere Hotelzimmer für seine Vorgesetzten buchen.

Hören Sie sich das Gespräch an und beantworten Sie die Fragen.

1. **Für wann möchte Arne die Zimmer buchen?**

   ____

2. **Wie viele Zimmer möchte er?**

   ____

3. **Welche Zimmer bietet das Hotel ihm an?**

   ____

4. **Wie viel kostet ein Einzelzimmer?**

   ____

5. **Wie heißt das Ausweichhotel?**

   ____

6. **Wie ist die Telefonnummer des Ausweichhotels?**

   ____

3. Office supplies

Mary Featherwood works at DFG Logistics in Norwich. She places an order for new stationery.

Listen to the conversation and fill in the order form.

Office Supplies Total

Customer: ____________________

Paper:
____ boxes of inkjet; size: ________

Labels:
____ packets; colour: ________

Envelopes:
Colour: ________ size: ________; amount: ________
Colour: ________ size: ________; amount: ________

Pens:
Colours: ____________________; ________ boxes at 80 per box

Delivery time: ____________

4. Preparing for a meeting

Das Bonner Büro von Worldwide IT Solutions Inc. erwartet Besuch aus den USA. Gerda Meier telefoniert mit ihrer Kollegin in den USA, weil sie den Konferenzraum vorbereiten möchte.

Hören Sie sich das Gespräch an und beantworten Sie die Fragen.

1. **Wen ruft Gerda an?**

   ____

2. **Was wird gebraucht?**

   ☐ Laptops ☐ USB-Sticks ☐ Computer-Mäuse ☐ CD-ROMs

3. **Wo soll das Mittagessen stattfinden?**

   ____

4. **Wieso isst Tyler keinen Kuchen?**

   ____

5. **Gegen was ist Danny allergisch?**

   ____

5. Problems with a delivery

Frank Neumeir nimmt einen Anruf entgegen. Ein Kunde aus Großbritannien beschwert sich über eine Lieferung.

Hören Sie sich das Telefonat an und beantworten Sie die Fragen auf Deutsch.

1. **Wie ist der Name des Kunden und seine Adresse?**

   ___

2. **Welche Referenznummer gibt der Kunde an?**

   ___

3. **Wie ist die Telefonnummer des Kunden?**

   ___

4. **Wie hat er bestellt und wann?**

   ___

5. **Was hat der Kunde bestellt?**

   ___

6. **Mit was droht der Kunde, falls das Problem nicht schnellstmöglich behoben wird?**

   ___

6. Telephone query

Michaela Hannhaus erhält einen Anruf von einem Zulieferer aus England.

Hören Sie sich das Gespräch an und beantworten Sie die Fragen bzw. kreuzen Sie die richtigen Antworten an.

1. **In welcher Abteilung von Morehouse-Communications arbeitet die Anruferin?**

   ☐ Personal

   ☐ Buchhaltung

   ☐ Marketing

   ☐ Vertrieb

   ☐ Einkauf

2. **Wen möchte Joanne Keele sprechen?**

   ___

3. **Was ist der Grund für ihre Beschwerde?**

   ___

4. **Welche Lösung schlägt Frau Hannhaus vor?**

   ___

5. **Wieso geht Joanne Keele davon aus, dass das Problem schnell geklärt wird?**

   ___

7. Stock control

Nicole Bergmann arbeitet in der Einkaufsabteilung eines Elektrounternehmens in Hagen. Sie möchte die Lagerbestände rechtzeitig vor Beginn des Weihnachtsgeschäftes auffüllen und spricht mit dem Lageristen des Depots in England.

Hören Sie sich das Gespräch an und beantworten Sie die Fragen.

Order

Name: ______________________

Niederlassung: ______________________

Geräte:

Modell: __________ Anzahl: __________ Preis: __________
Modell: __________ Anzahl: __________ Preis: __________
Modell: __________ Anzahl: __________ Preis: __________
Modell: __________ Anzahl: __________ Preis: __________
Modell: __________ Anzahl: __________ Preis: __________

Lieferung: ______________________

Sonstiges: ______________________

8. Email for you

Martin Böller from Cologne is doing work experience in the US office of the chemicals wholesaler he works for. While he is there he visits a seminar about effective emailing.

Listen to the talk and answer the questions.

1. **Who is giving the talk?**

____

____

2. **Why could receiving a lot of emails become a problem?**

____

____

3. **What measures does the speaker suggest for dealing with too many emails?**

____

____

4. **What are the dangers of email correspondence?**

____

____

9. Travel itinerary

Sandra Biegemann works for FitWorld, an international chain of fitness studios based in London. Her boss is planning to travel to the US to visit a few new studios there. She has asked Sandra to make the necessary travel arrangements.

Listen to Sandra's conversation with the travel company and fill in the travel itinerary.

Travel itinerary: Diane Kramer

Purpose of visit: ______________________

Day 1
Flight from: ____________ to: ______________
Departure: ____________ Arrival: ______________
Hotel: ______________
Appointments: none

Day 2
City: ______________
Appointments: Mark Davids, MidTown Gym, 4pm
Jean Middler, Central Gym, ____________
Betty Jones, ____________, ____________

Day 3
Flight from: ____________ to: Chicago
Departure: ____________ Arrival: ______________
Hotel: Grand Mid-Western
Appointments: Phil, Power Ladies Gym, ____________

Day 4
Flight from: Chicago to: ______________
Departure: ____________ Arrival: ______________
Hotel: ______________
Appointments: Denise, Get Fit, 6pm

Day 5
Flight from: ____________ to: ______________
Departure: ____________ Arrival: ______________

FitWorld

10. Finding a conference room

Mark Watkins, der Vertriebsleiter von Power Plastics in Süddeutschland, möchte in London einen Vortrag halten. Susanne Fanger, seine Assistentin, informiert sich über verfügbare Veranstaltungsräume.

Hören Sie sich die Telefongespräche an und machen Sie sich Notizen, indem Sie die Informationen ausfüllen.

Wo ist der Raum?		
Preis		
Personenzahl		
Verpflegung		
Welche Extras sind im Preis enthalten?		
Sonstiges		

11. Preparations for the trade fair

Martin Finke, Auszubildender bei Modern World, Cars and More, bereitet mit seinen amerikanischen Kollegen die Messe in Baltimore, USA, vor.

Hören Sie sich die Telefonkonferenz an und beantworten Sie die Fragen.

1. **Wann findet die Messe statt?**

   ____

2. **Wie viele Aussteller wird es geben?**

   ____

3. **Ab wann findet der Aufbau statt und wie viele Mitarbeiter werden benötigt?**

   ____

4. **Was schlägt Martin vor, um auf der Messe Aufsehen zu erregen?**

   ____

   ____

5. **Seit wann betreut Martins Kollege Thomas den Messeauftritt?**

   ____

6. **Wieso denkt Thomas, Martins Idee wird nicht funktionieren?**

   ____

   ____

12. Happy Sweets Plc

Melanie Wagner arbeitet für einige Monate im englischen Büro der Firma Happy Sweets Plc. Melanies Vorgesetzter bittet sie, mehrere Angebote von Frachtdienstleistern einzuholen, um eine dringende Lieferung nach Portugal zu schicken.

Hören Sie sich die Telefonate an und machen Sie sich Notizen, um die Angebote zu vergleichen. Achten Sie dabei auf:

- **Lieferzeiten**
- **Preis**
- **Versicherungsoptionen**
- **Garantien**

Welches ist das bessere Angebot?

___

13. Dealing with a complaint

Fredericke Wunderlich arbeitet bei Süße Träume, einer großen Kette von Bettenfachgeschäften. Sie nimmt eine Lieferung von Healthy Sleep aus Basingstoke entgegen und stellt Mängel fest.

Hören Sie sich Frau Wunderlichs Gespräch mit dem Lieferanten an und geben Sie kurz auf Deutsch wieder, was mit der Lieferung nicht stimmt.

___

___

___

___

14. Taking minutes

Simon Wölfe arbeitet bei der Glass AG in Flensburg. Er nimmt an einem Treffen mit amerikanischen, deutschen und englischen Managern teil. Simon soll nach dem Treffen ein kurzes Ergebnisprotokoll verfassen.

Hören Sie sich die Diskussion an und beantworten Sie die Fragen.

1. **Welchen Vorschlag macht George McFowler bezüglich der Zulieferer?**

   ___

2. **Wieso schlägt Anna Hanson vor, einige Fabriken zu schließen?**

   ___

3. **Was schlägt Chris Nettles, außer einem Einstellungsstopp, noch vor?**

   ___

4. **Welchen Grund, außer Kosten, gibt Chris Nettles für diesen Vorschlag an?**

   ___

5. **Wieso ist George McFowler der Ansicht, dass weniger Geld für Werbung ausgegeben werden kann?**

   ___

15. Job interview

Martin Smith has a job interview at Sintra Ltd. in Exeter. Betty Marsh, from the HR department, takes notes during the interview.

Listen to the interview and complete Betty's notes.

Sintra Ltd.

Full name of interviewee	
Present employment	
Current employer	
Reasons for wanting to leave current position	
Reasons for wanting to join Sintra Ltd.	
Language skills	
Mobility/flexibility	
Salary expectations	
Earliest date for commencement of job	

Sintra Ltd.

16. The new office

Sie haben gerade Ihr Praktikum im englischen Büro Ihrer Firma angefangen. Um Ihnen den Einstieg ein wenig zu erleichtern, gibt eine Kollegin Ihnen eine Broschüre über Bürobedarf und -einrichtungen.

How to equip your office

What kind of office equipment do you need?

If you plan to have your own office you need a lot of things. It makes sense to make a list of all the items you want to buy. You might need desks and chairs, bookshelves and computer equipment such as PCs, printers, scanners and monitors. It is also very useful to have a photocopier. To get in touch with the outside world you may use a telephone or a fax machine. For each individual workplace, usually people want to have a clock, a calendar, a letter tray, a waste paper basket, a hole punch, a stapler, a penholder and maybe a calculator. A lot of people like to have a picture frame with a photo of the family or a friend. And, of course, don't forget you'll need plenty of paper.

Welche Materialien bzw. Ausrüstung werden im Text erwähnt? Kreuzen Sie die Bilder an.

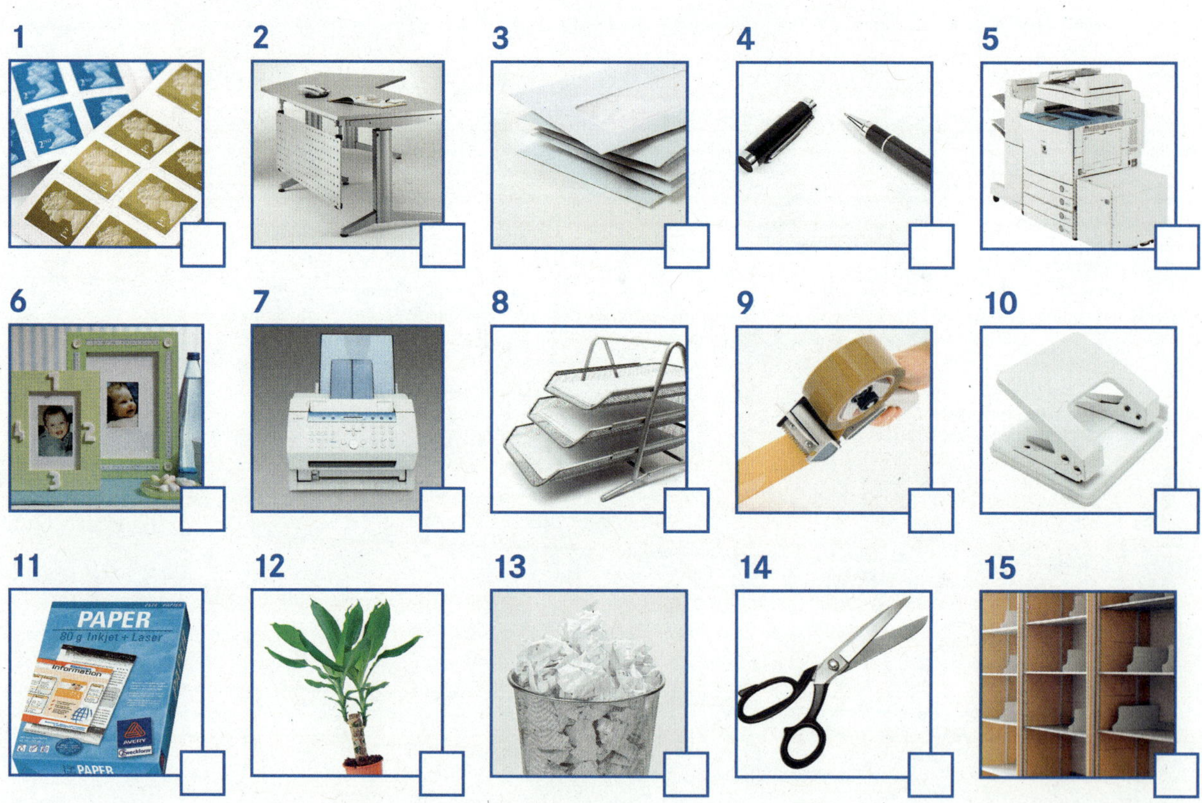

17. An order by telephone

Bringen Sie die Teile des Telefongesprächs in die richtige Reihenfolge. Tragen Sie dazu die Nummern 1 bis 12 in die Kästchen rechts ein.

- **a** You're welcome. Please hold the line, I'll put you through now. ☐
- **b** I'm afraid, Mr. Manson is out of the office today. Can I take a message? ☐
- **c** Good morning, EcoSystems London, Jim Donnelly speaking. How can I help you? ☐
- **d** Sanders, sales department. Good morning Ms. Myers. I heard you urgently need one of our products? ☐
- **e** Friday ... let me see. Yes, that's no problem. I'll make sure that the products leave the company today. ☐
- **f** Good morning. My name is Carol Myers from PowerTechnology. I would like to talk to Mr. Manson from the sales department. ☐
- **g** I don't know, the matter is rather urgent. We need one of your products very quickly. ☐
- **h** You're welcome. Goodbye. ☐
- **i** Yes, good morning Mrs. Sanders, that's right. Can I order five pieces of the FTG 2000? We need them next Friday. ☐
- **j** Thank you! ☐
- **k** Today? That's great! Thank you very much. Goodbye then. ☐
- **l** Oh, I see. I think I'll try to connect you to Mrs. Sanders, she is Mr. Manson's colleague. I'm sure she can help you. ☐

18. Job descriptions

Zur Vorbereitung auf ein Business-English-Seminar, das Ihre Firma anbietet, werden Sie von der Lehrerin gebeten, die folgende Aufgabe zu vervollständigen:

Match the job titles with the corresponding job descriptions:

1. Managing Director ☐
2. Personnel Manager ☐
3. Receptionist ☐
4. Sales Representative ☐
5. Purchasing Manager ☐
6. Secretary ☐
7. Marketing Manager ☐
8. Call Center Agent ☐
9. Finance Manager ☐

a This member of staff helps customers on the phone when they have questions.

b In this job, you are responsible for selling products to customers.

c The person is in charge of hiring employees, keeping personal files and advertising job vacancies.

d The person who heads the company. He/she is responsible for the whole company.

e Someone who types letters, keeps files, organizes meetings and sometimes also acts as a Personal Assistant and supports their boss in many ways.

f This person is responsible for payments, accounting and other matters where money is involved.

g Someone you usually find in the entrance area of a company greeting visitors and answering the phone.

h This person's area of responsibility is to launch advertising campaigns.

i This person is the head of the department which writes enquiries to suppliers, places orders and compares quotes.

19. Facts & figures

Lesen Sie diesen kurzen Bericht über die Firma Myers & Millers Soft Drinks International. Füllen Sie dann das unten stehende Faktenblatt aus.

Myers & Miller Soft Drinks International was founded 1967 in Sydney by Martin Myers. The company is one of the leading manufacturers of non-alcoholic drinks in Australia. They offer different juices and lemonades and have 15 different products altogether.
Their headquarters moved to Brisbane in 2001, but they have branches all over Australia and also in the USA and Canada. Starting with a staff of 20 in 1967, the company now has a workforce of approximately 11,000.
Myers & Miller mostly sell their products to wholesalers like supermarkets, hotels, restaurant chains. They also have large contracts with airlines and cruise ship companies. To make their brands well-known they sponsor big sporting events, produce TV commercials and send out promotion teams to give away free samples of their drinks.
Their turnover has grown every year. Last year, sales increased by 2.2% to 235,000,000 €.
Myers & Miller is still a private company, which is now headed by the founder's son, Brendan Myers.

Füllen Sie dieses Faktenblatt aus.

Produkte		**Werbung (Werbestrategien)**	
Hauptsitz		**Umsatz**	
Filialen		**Unternehmens-form**	
Mitarbeiter			
Kunden		**Geschäftsführer**	

20. Ordering online

You work in the customer relations department of a large insurance company in Scotland. Your company wants to buy some giveaways for customers. You are in charge of ordering the items online.

Put the steps of the online order procedure in the right order. Write the numbers 1 to 8 in the boxes on the right.

a) Usually, after your order has been processed, you will receive a confirmation email within a couple of minutes. ☐

b) If you have made a decision select your preferred item(s) from the catalogue. ☐

c) If there are any complaints about the products please contact us immediately. Otherwise we expect full payment within 10 days. ☐

d) We appreciate any feedback by mail, post or our website and hope we were able to satisfy you with our products. We are looking forward to serving you again. ☐

e) All of your chosen items are now in the shopping cart. Here you can review your entire order, delete certain items or change the quantity of a product. ☐

f) After this basic information, please choose the method of shipment and the terms of payment simply by clicking on it. Confirm the complete order and press the ORDER button. ☐

g) If the order has been confirmed, most of the ordered items will be shipped within 3 days and should arrive at your house within one week. ☐

h) If you reviewed the order and are sure about the items you want to order click "checkout". Then you have to fill in further details like your name, address, phone number and email address. ☐

21. How (not) to behave

Während Ihrer Mittagspause lesen Sie diesen Artikel in einem amerikanischen Magazin.

Study reveals 10 most terrible office behaviors

A co-worker who takes credit for someone else's work or tells obnoxious jokes is engaging in one of the top 10 most offensive workplace behaviors, according to survey results published this week. These and others appear on a "Terrible 10" list of rude working-world behaviors. While discrimination topped the list as most offensive, other highly ranked job-related violations occur beyond the office entrance, such as crazy driving.

"The research suggests that people are bothered more by the bad behavior of co-workers and strangers than by those of family and friends," said study team member P.M. Forni, director of the Civility Initiative at Johns Hopkins University.

Out of 30 examples of rude behavior, employees most often mentioned the following 10 as most offensive in this order:

- Discrimination in an employment situation.
- For commuters, aggressive driving that endangers others.
- Taking credit for someone else's work.
- Treating service providers as inferiors.
- Jokes or remarks that make fun of somebody, including remarks about race, gender, age, disability, sexual preference and religion.
- Children who behave aggressively or who bully others.
- Littering or spitting.
- Misuse of handicapped privileges.
- Smoking in non-smoking places or smoking in front of non-smokers without asking.
- Using cell phones or text messaging in conversations or during an appointment or meeting.

For this survey, Forni and his colleagues asked 615 employees of two companies in Baltimore, along with employees and students at the University of Baltimore, in May 2007. The participants rated 30 examples of rude behavior from 1 (not offensive) to 5 (most offensive).

After you have read the text, decide which answers are correct and cross the boxes accordingly. Decide between YES or NO or choose between multiple statements. Only one statement is correct.

Yes No

1. ☐ ☐ According to the study, workers suffer more from bad behavior of their colleagues or people they don't know than from family and friends.

2. The participants

☐ could choose between 30 different descriptions of bad behavior.
☐ could choose between "not offensive" and "most offensive".
☐ had to rate 10 different examples of bad behavior.

3. Which of the situations below describe one of the most terrible office behaviors of the top ten list?

Yes No

a ☐ ☐ People who have to use their car to get to work drive too slowly.
b ☐ ☐ Colleagues who borrow money but don't give it back.
c ☐ ☐ A colleague smokes without asking if it's okay.
d ☐ ☐ A colleague pretends that he/she has completed a task at work but it was actually someone else who did it.
e ☐ ☐ Colleagues make "funny" remarks about people who are old or disabled.
f ☐ ☐ People don't throw their garbage in the intended "boxes".
g ☐ ☐ Work is interrupted by mobile phone conversations.

4. For this study they asked

☐ the staff of 615 companies in Baltimore.
☐ working people and students from Baltimore.
☐ 615 employees, university staff and students from Baltimore.

22. Business travel

Noise levels on trains, planes and in airport lounges are increasing and it's stressing you out

Gone are the days when a long train journey was ideal for catching up on work or just letting your brain wander over those great ideas it never had time to have. Noise levels in public spaces are sky-rocketing with the growth of loud mobile phone calls, iPods, and mobile internet access, letting people view sites like YouTube while on the move.
Some cities are taking action to protect our eardrums and our sanity. Stockholm has just introduced mobile phone free zones on all its buses, trains and subways. A city spokesperson said the move was driven by "the need for peace and quiet when travelling" as well as criticism of travellers who speak too loudly on public transport, upsetting others.
If other cities follow, increasing numbers of business travellers would breathe a sigh of relief as they recognise that increasing noise is ramping up their stress levels and reducing their ability to work during their travels.
Dr Deepak Prasher, professor of audiology at University College, London, said: "The noise level in public places is going up. There are very few places you can go now for absolute peace and quiet."
Noise readings in trains carried out by UCL found sound levels as high as 105 decibels – much higher than the 85 decibel level at which UK workplaces must provide hearing protection. Dr Prasher said: "Our measurement of noise in the Underground is very high indeed."
There is a bank of evidence that high noise levels affect concentration and attention. Research shows noise and stress are very much related, said Dr Prasher. "Noise has an impact on health generally," he added.
While some train companies have attempted to address the problem with "quiet" carriages, anyone who has travelled in one of these designated coaches soon finds that there are plenty of fellow passengers who will happily ignore the signs, and little sign of enforcement from train staff.
As external noise on trains - such as clanking of machinery - has become quieter, noise from other passengers has grown, said Dr Prasher.
Like many other regular business travellers, Kudlak has his fingers crossed that the last bastion of peace, one of the few places you can escape from the boss's calls, is not destroyed. "Right now the airplane is the only place I can relax and work offline."
But while Kudlak acknowledged his stress levels were suffering, he reckoned sometimes the only way to deal with other people's noise is to switch on the phone and join in.
One airline employee, who declined to be named, said: "God help us if they allow mobile phone use in the air." Can you imagine the dialogue: "We are now circling over London, I can see the house."
These travellers are not alone: a study by the Association of Flight Attendants found most air passengers did not want the ban on phone calls in-flight lifted.

a) Decide whether the following statements are true or false:

Statement	True	False
a) A train journey is ideal for catching up on work or just letting your brain wander		
b) In Stockholm it is not allowed to use mobile phones on public transport		
c) The noise readings of University College London found that the sound levels in trains are almost as high as the allowed figures		
d) Rail companies have reacted to the noise problem i. e. with low noise machinery		
e) Passengers increase noise levels rather than keeping quiet and being considerate		

b) Answer the following questions according to the text.

1. **Is it allowed to use mobile phones on airplanes?**

2. **What do the majority of flight passengers want as far as the use of mobile phones is concerned?**

3. **Which effect do high noise levels have?**

23. Working conditions

You work in the Human Resources Department of an international chemicals company. Some employees will be transferred to the subsidiary in Dubai and you have been asked to find some information about salaries and general working conditions there, to answer their questions.

Working in Dubai

Salaries in Dubai are usually similar to, or greater than those paid in western countries. But because the region has no personal taxation, net income is usually much greater, which is one of the major attractions of working in Dubai. In the past, the payment was split into various elements: basic salary, extra money for a car or housing, medical cover, education for children and air tickets for home visits. Today, however, employers tend just to pay a salary, which covers all these expenses, although in some cases there are bonuses.
In addition to their salary, contract workers are awarded an 'indemnity' at the end of the contract period. The indemnity is usually based on basic salary excluding any bonuses. The indemnity can be a significant amount of money if you've been working in Dubai for a long time, and many people manage either to save an amount of money or to live the high life. If you're clever and disciplined, you should be able to do some of both. The indemnity is an end-of-contract bonus which is required by law to be paid to foreign workers as a sort of 'thank you' for being of service to the state. (It's also known as 'end of service benefits'.) Indemnity payments usually are 15 (in some cases 20) days of basic pay per year of employment for the first three years and thereafter a month's salary per year of employment. Note that some Arab companies regularly delay the payment of salaries. In this event, you have little alternative but to wait.

Working Hours & Overtime

The working week in Dubai tends to vary between 40 and 48 hours, depending on the particular company's policy. Office hours are usually from 8.30 or 9am to 5.30 or 6pm. There are no differences in time-keeping between summer and winter. In the month of Ramadan, the working day is reduced to six hours. Legally this should apply to all staff, but many companies only apply it to Muslims, who fast during daylight hours. Friday is the Muslim day of rest and, if your company has a five-day working week, the other day off will probably be either Thursday or Saturday. Saturday is the more popular choice for international companies, as taking Thursday off would mean a reduction in the number of working days that are the same as the rest of the world. On the other hand, some companies insist on Thursday as being the day off, as the school 'weekend' is Thursday and Friday.

Answer your colleagues' questions.

1. **Do salaries consist of different parts, like basic pay, medical cover and so on?**
2. **Can you use the indemnity payment only to save money?**
3. **Do companies in Dubai always pay their employees on time?**
4. **If I work in Dubai for eight years, will I receive an indemnity of 15-20 days of basic pay per year?**
5. **Are the "weekends" for international companies usually Fridays and Saturdays?**
6. **Do pupils and students have their "weekends" on Thursday and Friday?**

Tick the correct statements according to the text:

1. People in western countries still mostly earn more than in Dubai. ☐
   It is advantageous to work in Dubai because they often grant performance or other bonuses. ☐
   Since there are no personal taxes in Dubai, people have a higher income in general. ☐
   In the past, employers in Dubai paid much higher salaries than nowadays. ☐
2. If your contract ends in Dubai, employers will usually reward you with a certificate. ☐
   The longer you have been working for an employer, the higher your indemnity payment is at the end of every year. ☐
   Basic salary and bonuses determine the amount of your indemnity. ☐
   According to the law, indemnity payments have to be paid to employees who fulfilled their contracts. ☐
3. Work usually starts early in Dubai: between 5.30 and 6pm. ☐
   In winter, employees work one hour longer than in summer. ☐
   A six-hour working day is usual in Dubai. ☐
   Muslims only have to work six hours per day during Ramadan. ☐

24. Ordering office supplies

Your company is looking for a new office items supplier. You received an advertising brochure about membership with Costco.

Prepare the most important information about the company and the membership in the following tables to present to your colleagues and to make the decision easier.

Why Become A Costco Member?

We are a membership warehouse club, dedicated to bringing our members the best possible prices on quality brand-name merchandise. The company's first location, opened in 1976 under the Price Club name, was in a converted airplane hangar on Morena Boulevard in San Diego. Originally serving only small businesses, the company found it could achieve far greater success by also serving a selected audience of non-business members. With that change, the growth of the warehouse club industry was off and running. In 1983, the first Costco warehouse location was opened in Seattle. Costco became the first company ever to grow from zero to $3 billion in sales in less than six years. When Costco and Price Club merged in 1993, the combined company, operating under the name PriceCostco, had 206 locations generating $16 billion in annual sales. Our operating philosophy has been simple. Keep costs down and pass the savings on to our members. Our large membership base and tremendous buying power, combined with our never-ending quest for efficiency, result in the best possible prices for our members. Since resuming the Costco name in 1997, the company has grown worldwide with total sales in recent years exceeding $50 billion.

Executive Membership

Executive Membership is our highest level of membership. Executive Members receive an annual 2% reward on most Costco purchases, and extra benefits on member services, such as lower prices on auto financing.

Business Membership

Business Membership is available to all licensed businesses, non-profit organizations, government agencies. The $50 annual membership fee includes one household card. Additional Business Membership cards are available for $40 each. Business identification (business license, resale certificate, or three pieces of business ID) is required when applying for Business Membership. Business Members who wish to purchase for resale must provide the Costco warehouse membership counter with the appropriate resale information.

Gold Star Membership

Gold Star Membership is available for individuals who do not qualify for a Business Membership. The Gold Star Membership is $50 per year, which includes one household card. See the membership counter at your warehouse for additional information, or call us at 1-800-774-2678.

Fill in the requested information from the text in the tables below.
In the first table you should concentrate on the development of the company from the beginning.
(If the text doesn't give any information, leave a blank.)

year	step in company development/ name of company at that time	location(s) of company	annual sales

Types of membership

	benefits	target group/category	membership fee
Executive			
Business			
Gold Star			

25. A job in the USA

Nach Ihrer Ausbildung wollen Sie in den USA arbeiten, um Ihre Sprachkenntnisse zu verbessern. Sie haben einige Stellenangebote gefunden und vergleichen sie nun übersichtsartig, um sich einen Überblick zu verschaffen.

Füllen Sie dazu die Tabelle aus.

Office Assistant
OFFICO, Inc.
Headquarters
Chicago, IL 60606

We are a leading wholesaler of office items and are currently hiring a temporary full time Office Assistant. Qualified candidates should have strong organizational and accounting skills, and at least 1 year experience in an office environment. Your daily job is to answer customer enquiries by phone and mail, accounting and writing orders. Extensive knowledge of Microsoft Office required. Must have a reliable car for errands. Pay Rate $10–$14/hour. If you are professional and looking for an exciting opportunity and are willing to work at weekends, please call Bernard Smythe for a telephone interview at 386-3440.

General Office Clerk
Summers & Sons
1020 10th Street
Modesto, CA 95354

Local car dealer in Modesto is seeking a Spanish speaking skilled General Office Clerk for part-time indefinite employment. You will be responsible for answering phones, making appointments, filing, faxing, copying. You are expected to be trained for the use of MS Excel and have a High School Diploma. Base pay is $11 per hour, an increase is possible after further education we offer. You have to be prepared to work very flexible hours and overtime if required. If you are up for a challenge, and ready to build your office skills, write an application to our personnel manager Mr. Kilter!

Office Assistant
Mirana Ltd.
165 Broadway
New York,
NY 10006-1400

Software Company seeks an administrative assistant for indefinite employment. You should be able to arrange meetings and travel plans, organize fairs and perform general office duties.
In this full-time job you should be highly organized and able to work in a fast paced environment.
Occasional business trips are required.
This growing, well-known, stable organization offers a competitive salary of $11-15 and pension plan.
Email your application to our HR Manager, Val James at val.james@sid-wvd.com.

	1 OFFICO	2 Summers & Sons	3 MIRANA
Branche			
Dauer des Vertrages			
Arbeitsumfang (Vollzeit/ Teilzeit)			
Arbeitsort			
Kontaktmöglichkeit für Bewerbung			
Stundenlohn			
Tätigkeiten			
besondere Fähigkeiten/ Erfahrung/ Abschlüsse, die man mitbringen sollte			
Leistungen für die Mitarbeiter			
Besonderheiten der Stelle			

26. Career choice: secretary

Sie informieren sich in einer amerikanischen Zeitschrift über verschiedene Berufe. Dabei stoßen Sie auf den folgenden Artikel.

Sie wollen einigen Kollegen über den Artikel Auskunft geben. Halten Sie dafür die wichtigsten Punkte des Artikels stichwortartig auf Deutsch fest.

A day in the life of a secretary

A secretary manages information. Responsibilities can run from scheduling staff appointments to office management to managing an entire database. Since the computer is central to any modern office, mastery of the latest office technology is essential. Secretaries are often the primary conduit of information from their employers to the rest of the world, so they must be comfortable communicating with others in person and on the telephone. Secretaries who work in specialized fields, such as law and accounting, have a working knowledge of that field. Executive secretaries often initiate and execute independent projects. One secretary we spoke to described her view of keeping busy after accomplishing a day's assignments well before the deadline: "You can bury your nose in a magazine, or you can find something constructive to do. Good secretaries are self-starters." Few professions call for such careful execution of so many specialized tasks. Such professionalism combined with the almost constant changes in business technology has led secretaries to turn to one another for support, training, and solidarity. "You often don't know exactly what's expected of you," remarked one secretary. "It's easier if there are other secretaries there to help you clarify things, especially in a place like a law office." Because so much of the job depends on organization, secretaries' skills are really tested when they work for particularly disorganized bosses. "Your main task is making sure everything goes smoothly, anticipating as well as accomplishing particular tasks." And secretaries are still expected to handle their employers' moods and foibles in the course of everyday business. The best advice we heard: "Be prepared for anything."

Paying your dues

Some of the clerical skills expected of secretaries can be picked up on the job, but secretarial candidates should have already mastered typing and word processing in high school, college, or vocational school. Competition in the field allows employers to place greater demands on applicants: A college education is a valuable asset. In a global economy, being bilingual or even trilingual is often a plus. Stenography has become something of a lost art, but it may come in handy with an old-fashioned boss.

Associated careers

"Secretary" is an umbrella term for any number of administrative jobs, and the best-qualified secretaries have mastered them all. Many secretaries use their experience to enter a particular profession. Some secretaries get practice using editorial skills and move into editorial jobs. Many secretaries who are responsible for office management, including payrolls, bookkeeping, bill-paying and maintenance of the office's physical plant, find more specialized opportunities in these areas. Those interested in doing secretarial work on a temporary basis may seek assignments through a temporary agency. These agencies provide companies with administrative workers on a daily, weekly, or monthly basis. Temp work has the advantages of flexibility and variety – of bosses, office settings, and tasks. It also has the drawbacks of sameness – you will quite possibly be given one boring task to do for a week – and the possibility that the work may dry up at certain times of the year when you could really use a paycheck.

Aufgabenbereiche:	
Ausbildung:	
erforderliche Kenntnisse (z. B. Software):	
Chancen für berufliche Weiterentwicklung:	
Vor- und Nachteile von Zeit-/Leiharbeit:	

Eine Ihrer Kolleginnen, die den Artikel auch gelesen hat, bittet Sie, ihr die folgenden Begriffe kurz auf Deutsch zu erklären (im Text unterstrichen):

1. **"mastery of the latest office technology"**

2. **"Secretaries are often the primary conduit of information"**

3. **"Good secretaries are self-starters."**

4. **"is an umbrella term"**

27. New ways in advertising

Sie arbeiten in der Werbeabteilung eines großen internationalen Unternehmens. Den folgenden Artikel haben Sie in einer Fachzeitschrift entdeckt. Da Sie der Ansicht sind, er könnte für einige Ihrer Kunden interessant sein, wollen Sie ein kurzes Merkblatt erstellen.

Marketers hail the mobile phone as advertising's promised land

ADVERTISING on mobile phones is a tiny business. Last year spending on mobile ads was $871m worldwide according to Informa Telecoms & Media, a research firm, compared with $24 billion spent on internet advertising and $450 billion spent on all advertising. But marketing wizards are beginning to talk about it with the sort of hyperbole they normally reserve for products they are paid to sell. It is destined, some say, to supplant not only internet advertising, but also television, radio, print and billboards, the four traditional pillars of the business.

At the moment, most mobile advertising takes the form of text messages. But telecoms firms are also beginning to deliver ads to handsets alongside video clips, web pages, and music and game downloads, through mobiles that permit such things. Informa forecasts that annual expenditure will reach $11.4 billion by 2011. Other analysts predict the market will be as big as $20 billion by then.

The 2.5 billion mobile phones around the world can potentially reach a much bigger audience than the planet's billion or so personal computers. The number of mobile phones in use is also growing much faster than the number of computers, especially in poorer countries. Better yet, most people carry their mobile with them everywhere – something that cannot be said of television or computers.

Yet the biggest selling point of mobile ads is what marketing types call "relevance". Advertisers believe that about half of all traditional advertising does not reach the right audience. Less effort (and money) is wasted with online advertising: half of it is sold on a "pay-per-click" basis, which means advertisers pay only when consumers click on an ad. But mobile advertising through text messages is the most focused: if marketers use mobile firms' profiles of their customers cleverly enough, they can tailor their advertisements to match each subscriber's habits.

One problem might be that consumers are used to ads on television and radio and they consider their mobiles a more personal device. A flood of advertising might offend its audience, and thus undermine its own value. Tolerance of advertising also differs from one market to another. In the Middle East, for example, unsolicited text messages are quite common, and do not prompt many complaints. But subscribers might not prove so open-minded in Europe or America.

Another hitch, says Nicky Walton-Flynn of Informa, is that operators have lots of databases with information about their clients' habits that would be of great interest to advertisers. But privacy laws may prevent them from sharing it. Moreover, advertisers, operators and middlemen have not agreed a common format for this information, nor worked out how to share the revenue it might yield.

Some think these obstacles will confine mobile advertising to a niche for years to come. But others see a whole new world of possibilities, as more people use their phones to access the internet and consumers grow used to the intrusion. Mobile phones, some of which are now equipped with satellite-positioning technology, could be used to alert people to the charms of stores or restaurants they are walking or driving past.

Tying ads to online searches from mobile phones is another potential goldmine. A subscriber typing in "pizza" for instance, could receive ads for nearby pizza parlours along with his generic search results. Such a customer, mobile operators hope, is likely to be more grateful than annoyed by the intrusion. What could be more relevant than that?

Merkblatt: Mobiltelefonwerbung	
Größe des Markts:	
Art der Werbung:	
potenzielle Wirkung:	
Vorteile:	
Nachteile:	

Erklären Sie die folgende Aussage auf Deutsch:

Some think these obstacles will confine mobile advertising to a niche for years to come.

28. A modern way to get a job

Eine Bekannte von Ihnen hat sich auf eine Stelle in Australien beworben. Sie wird zu einem Video-Interview eingeladen und bittet Sie um Hilfe bei der Vorbereitung.

Lesen Sie den Artikel und beantworten Sie kurz die Fragen Ihrer Bekannten.

Video Interviews - The modern way to interview

Increasingly companies are recruiting from all over the world. Interviewing methods have changed to incorporate video conferencing and telephone interviews. Using these cost effective methods of interviewing saves time and resources and allows employers to consider applicants from outside their own geographical location.

Video Conferencing

Video conferencing gives you the opportunity to apply for jobs, even if you can't fly to the other side of the world at short notice for a face-to-face interview. It's a great way of making an impact on a future employer and they can also get a sense of what you are capable of. You can express enthusiasm, focus and commitment better than you could in a telephone interview. You can also respond more directly to their questions.

Practice at home with a camcorder so you can see if you have any off-putting habits such as touching your hair or putting your hand over your mouth. Think about the best position to sit in that looks professional and friendly but is still comfortable for you. Don't get preoccupied with how the technology works, focus on what you're trying to achieve and getting your key points across to the interviewer.

Dress as you would if you were going to a face-to-face interview. Avoid light colours or patterns as it may be difficult for the camera to focus. The interviewer may not be able to see all of you but you'll feel more confident if you're dressed to impress. Sit up straight and try not to move around too much as the camera will be positioned on you.

Find out beforehand where the interview is going to be held and how long it will take you to get there, get there in plenty of time so that you can get comfortable and make sure all the equipment is working. Speak to the company providing the video conferencing facilities and find out who to contact if there is a problem and whether a technician will be on hand if you should run into difficulties. During some video conferences the video monitor may show an image of you, as well as the interviewer. This can be distracting so find out before the interview starts how to turn it off. Make sure you know who is initiating the call and, if you are dialling out, what number to use. Take a notepad and pen with you, don't be afraid to take notes if you feel it is appropriate but don't become distracted. Have a copy of your résumé and the job description to refer to but don't read from them.

As with all interviews, research the company before the interview. Find out as much information as possible about the company, department and the role that you're being interviewed for. The internet is a very good source of information and sites such as Google News will have details of any recent press coverage. It is essential that you look at the company's website. This is a vital source of information and may contain information such as the Annual Report – this can often be downloaded from the website. Make sure you have excellent market knowledge and are aware of any issues affecting the industry and company. Read industry magazines and the business pages of broadsheet newspapers to make sure you know of any relevant media coverage. Most newspapers will have an online archive that you can search.

Make sure you understand the whole recruitment process. Who will be interviewing you? What is the next stage? Do they require references? Don't be afraid to ask questions.

You will be able to see the interviewer on the video monitor, so as you would with a face-to-face interview, maintain eye contact. Treat the interview as a normal conversation, keep your head up and try to remain natural. Be aware of your body language. Keep your hand and body movements to a minimum and make sure you're sitting in a comfortable position. Jerky or rapid movements can look distorted on a video monitor.

Even with the most sophisticated video-conferencing technology there will be slight time delays, this can be quite disconcerting for the first time user. Leave lots of pauses before talking to allow all your words to be relayed to the interviewer. Try to remain calm and confident and resist the temptation to fill the void. ...

...
Be positive! Smile!
If you've answered a question negatively try to turn it into a positive. For example, "I'm not naturally patient with people who are slow to learn. However, I realise this and take extra time now to explain things to people as simply as possible."
If asked why you want to leave your current role make your response positive. Never criticise a past employer.
If you are unable to answer a question when prompted, ask if you can go back to it at a later stage. Let the interviewer know if you are interested in the job. If you are enthusiastic it could make you stand out above the others. The company will know that it's worth their while progressing things with you.

1. **Wie kann man sich auf das Video-Interview vorbereiten?**

2. **Muss man bei der Kleiderwahl etwas Besonderes beachten?**

3. **Muss man die Technik selbst bedienen können?**

4. **Kann ich während des Gesprächs Notizen machen?**

5. **Soll ich viele Gesten benutzen, um das, was ich sage, zu unterstützen?**

6. **Was soll ich machen, wenn es Zeitverzögerungen gibt?**

7. **Was tue ich, wenn mir keine positive Antwort einfällt?**

8. **Soll ich jede Frage beantworten, auch wenn ich die Antwort nicht weiß?**

29. Tips for working abroad

Sie denken darüber nach, nach Ihrer Ausbildung für einige Zeit im Ausland zu arbeiten. Daher interessieren Sie sich für den folgenden Artikel.

The number of professionals of working age who decide to spend a period of time working abroad is on the increase annually.
Many people believe a time overseas will not only broaden their cultural horizons but potentially improve their ongoing career prospects as well – if you too are planning on working abroad here are our top five tips for a successful relocation overseas and an easy transition into a new work place.

1

The country you choose to move to might depend on your profession and the ability to find suitable employment there – alternatively, if you're looking only for employment every now and then your country choice options may be far broader. Whichever country you choose you need to consider the likely employment prospects available and the living expenses of that country in relation to the amount you can realistically earn.

2

Depending on the country you come from and the one in which you'd now like to work, certain visas, permits, permissions and approval may be required to enter the country, live there and take up a job. Make sure you check out all the requirements before deciding for a country and find out whether it'll be easier for you to get all your permissions if you have an offer of employment already. If this is the case then you would be best advised to find suitable employment before you move to the other country.

3

In some countries many standard university and further education qualifications are accepted. But that's not the case in all countries, so you might have to translate your qualifications. Alternatively you may have to apply to have your qualifications recognised or to take examinations or practical tests to show your skills.
If you require certain qualifications and permissions to run your professional business, ensure you check out the rules for your trade in the country you're interested in moving to.

4

Some companies pay you fully back for all your relocation expenses and may even offer classes and ongoing support and assistance to help make the move abroad that much easier for the entire family. Moving abroad will be a stressful experience – there are no two ways about it – so make sure you accept all the help on offer. That way your own experience of working and living abroad will be that much more pleasant.

5

Don't forget that some countries have a different tax structure. Check out the rates of tax you'll have to pay for based on the country you're interested in moving to and the salary you can expect to earn. Remember that as a foreigner you're able to use all the tax breaks offered in your new country of residence and you may also be entitled to more breaks especially if you have to support two households. As a foreigner you may also be able to benefit from the world of investing and banking and this is an area you should take a little time to explore as it could allow you to save yourself tax and have more money to spend on enjoying your new life abroad.

Decide whether the following statements are true or false.

Statement	True	False
1. Every year more and more people go abroad to work.		
2. There are companies which pay the costs of your move.		
3. It can be very stressful to accept the help which is offered when you move.		
4. In most other countries you will have to deal with additional taxes which reduce your salary.		
5. Since you are not a native speaker it doesn't make much sense to invest time in investing and banking.		

Answer the following questions:

1. Why do people go abroad to work?

2. Which aspects do you have to consider when you decide for a country to move to?

3. Name the kind of documents you might need if you want to travel to a country and to live there!

4. What about your qualifications when you go abroad? Are they fully accepted?

30. Business meetings

As the new personal assistant to the personnel manager you are in charge of organising regular meetings. As the last meetings haven't been satisfactory, you search for ways to improve them. Your proposals are expected at the next staff meeting. The following text was recommended to you by a colleague.

How to Run an Effective Business Meeting

How productive are your business meetings? Many studies have shown that more time is wasted in meetings than in any other business activity. It is estimated that people spend 20-40% (upper management is much more) of their time in meetings and that meetings are only 44-50% efficient (source: Steve Kaye). By improving the efficiency of your next meeting, you may increase your results.

The first step in improving the efficiency of your business meetings is to recognize that meetings are a collaborative effort. The very definition of a meeting is a TEAM activity where SELECT people gather to perform WORK that requires GROUP effort. All participants of a meeting, therefore, must play a role in remaining focused and progressing through the meeting in a timely manner.

Before calling a meeting, it must first be decided whether it is necessary. Remember a meeting is not always the most effective way. Other options available might be sending a memo or an email. It is the responsibility of the chairperson to determine the need for calling the meeting and who should attend. In general, it is best to invite as few participants as possible (key players only).

Effective meetings need leadership. Leading a meeting requires attention, confidence, creativity, diplomacy, empathy, flexibility, wits, toughness and yes, humor! The primary role of the leader is to establish the ground rules for the meeting which are namely: to minimize confusion and disruptions and to institute a code of conduct. Some examples of team game rules that are designed to make meetings more effective are:

1. If you are planning to introduce a proposal or discuss an issue in a group meeting, send out any relevant information to all team members several days before the meeting.
2. Review the agenda and bring any relevant materials with you to the meeting so that the group can make informed decisions.
3. Don't try to influence a few members before the meeting and try to surprise the rest of the group in a "surprise attack" with an idea.
4. Come to the meetings on time.
5. If you are going to be absent, inform others beforehand and send a stand-in who can make at least some decisions in your name.
6. Focus on listening and seeking understanding before disagreeing.
7. If you are the minute keeper, distribute complete and accurate minutes to everyone within 48 hours of the meeting.
8. If you agree to something, do what you say you will do. Be accountable to each other.
9. Sarcasm, personal attacks, interrupting, dominating the discussion, or engaging in distracting behavior during a meeting are all non-productive behaviors. Agree not to engage in them.
10. It is okay to disagree during a meeting, but once the group has made a decision, it needs to be supported by everyone outside of the meeting. Passive resistance, sabotage, negative gossip and guerrilla warfare are not okay.
11. Remember to celebrate successes and to thank members for their efforts.

In addition to implementing these concepts, an effective meeting leader must enforce a code of conduct in order to maintain a safe environment for discussing ideas. The chairperson should ask the meeting attendees to follow some simple guidelines to ensure an orderly meeting such as respect others, work as a team, no rank in the room and so on.

It is as equally important to end a meeting efficiently as it is to conduct it. Besides just ending a business meeting on time there should be a review of agenda items and results, as well as assignments. A set agenda for the next meeting should also be prepared.

1. Explain in your own words: "remaining focused and progressing through the meeting in a timely manner".

2. What is considered as a "key player"?

3. What are the most important functions of the chairperson?

4. Which behaviour patterns should be avoided during a meeting?

5. Describe what is meant by a "surprise attack".

Statement	True	False
1. Estimates show that only about half of the time you spend in meetings is effective.		
2. Alternative options for calling a meeting are writing a memo or an email.		
3. If you are planning to discuss a topic or make a proposal in a meeting, do not hesitate to make it spontaneously.		
4. If you cannot go to a meeting, apologise in advance.		
5. Passive resistance is only acceptable outside the meeting		
6. One important meeting guideline is that it doesn't matter what rank the people in the meeting have.		

1. Writing about work

Sie wollen an einem Business-Englisch-Kurs teilnehmen, den Ihr Unternehmen anbietet. Die Kursleiterin bittet Sie, zur ersten Unterrichtsstunde einen kurzen Text auf Englisch über Ihren derzeitigen Arbeitsplatz mitzubringen.

Beschreiben Sie Ihre derzeitige berufliche Situation.
Gehen Sie dabei auf typische Arbeitsvorgänge und Tagesabläufe ein.

2. Office party

Sie arbeiten in einem internationalen Unternehmen. Einmal im Jahr findet eine abteilungsübergreifende Feier an einem der internationalen Standorte statt. Dieses Jahr wird die Feier in London stattfinden. Ihr Vorgesetzter in London teilt Ihnen mit, dass die Feier verschoben werden muss und es einige Änderungswünsche bezüglich der Bewirtung gibt.

Schreiben Sie eine E-Mail an die Firma, die die Feier organisiert, und teilen Sie die Änderungswünsche mit. Beachten Sie dabei folgende Punkte, die Ihnen Ihr Vorgesetzter genannt hat:

- **refer to booking of 15th September**
- **express apologies for postponing the order and the trouble caused**
- **fixed date: 30th March, new date: 30th May**
- **changes to the menu:**

former items on the menu	new items on the menu
40 veal cutlets	60 veal cutlets
100 sausages	85 sausages
—	30 salmon steaks
80 chicken drumsticks	120 chicken drumsticks

- **rest of the menu remains the same**
- **ask for new prices and confirmation**

An: butcherspartyfever@yahoo-wvd.com

Cc:

Betreff: Our booking, 15th September

3. Writing an order

You are on a work placement in Bristol. You work in the office of a large removal company called Movies. Your colleague asks you to place an order for some equipment with a supplier in Bournemouth.

Read your colleague's note and use her instructions to write the order on a separate piece of paper.

NOTE

Subject: *Order for equipment*

Please order the following items:
30 silver doorstops
20 black straps at 5 metres each
25 blue straps at 10 metres each
60 beige boxes (58cm x 75cm x 47cm)
150 white boxes (30cm x 40cm x 50cm)
50 grey boxes (45cm x 30cm x 65cm)
25 grey locks
35 black combination locks

Ask for delivery as soon as possible and whether they can send the new catalogue for this year.
Many thanks.

4. Discover Dresden

Sie arbeiten bei Imagination, einer großen Werbeagentur in Dresden. Ihre Vorgesetzte möchte die britischen Kunden der Agentur nach Dresden einladen. Sie bittet Sie, die Einladung an die Kunden zu verfassen.

Schreiben Sie die Einladung.

Folgende Stichpunkte sollen Ihnen dabei helfen:

- **Einladung nach Dresden als Dank für die bisherige Zusammenarbeit**
- **Programm: Tag 1: Anreise, gemeinsames Abendessen im Pulverturm; Tag 2: Stadtführung; Tag 3: Besuch der weltberühmten Meissener Porzellan-Manufaktur; Tag 4: Abreise**
- **Termin: 9. bis 12. Mai**
- **Unterbringung in komfortablem Hotel im Dresdner Stadtzentrum auf Kosten der Agentur**
- **Bitte um Anmeldung bis 1. April**

5. Booking a hotel room

Your company, P&T Textiles, offers a work exchange programme and you have been given the opportunity to participate. You are now working in P&T Textile's Glasgow office.

Your boss there asks you to book some hotel rooms in London during the next fashion week. Write an email including the following details:

- **book 3 single rooms with shower from 18 to 22 October.**
- **half-board, 2 people are vegetarians**
- **arrival late in the evening, 24 hour check-in? (could not find any information on the Internet)**
- **book the hotel's small conference room for 21 October, from 6 to 8 pm**
- **ask when payment due**
- **ask for confirmation**

6. Writing an enquiry

Sie sind Sekretär/-in bei Office Exquisite, einem Büromöbelhersteller in Frankfurt. Ihre Vorgesetzte bittet Sie, eine Anfrage an ein amerikanisches Unternehmen, das als Geschäftspartner infrage käme, zu verfassen.

Berücksichtigen Sie dabei die folgenden Punkte:

- **Adresse des Unternehmens im Internet gefunden**
- **Informationen zu eigenem Unternehmen geben:**
  - **führender Hersteller von exquisiten Büromöbeln mit Sitz in Frankfurt, Filiale in München**
  - **seit fünf Jahren erfolgreich europaweit tätig**
  - **jetzt Markteinführung auf dem amerikanischen Markt für das nächste Jahr geplant**
  - **anspruchsvolle Geschäftspartner gesucht**
- **eigenen Katalog für Überblick beifügen**
- **Freude über baldige Antwort ausdrücken**

Schreiben Sie die Anfrage, die Adresse des amerikanischen Unternehmens ist
Office Universe, 348 Riverwalk, Pewaukee, WI 53072, USA

7. Reply to an enquiry

Sie arbeiten in der Einkaufsabteilung einer großen Druckerei. Sie erhielten eine Anfrage eines großen Papierlieferanten aus England, der sich eine Zusammenarbeit wünscht.

Schreiben Sie eine Antwort auf die Anfrage und beachten Sie dabei folgende Punkte:

- **Dank für die Anfrage ausdrücken**
- **sehr großes Interesse an den Produkten und an einer Geschäftsbeziehung bekunden**
- **Gibt es Mengenrabatt?**
- **Lieferzeiten und Lieferbedingungen erfragen, ebenfalls Zahlungsbedingungen**
- **freundlicher Schlusssatz**

8. The new TX7

Sie arbeiten am Empfang im Autohaus „Hachenberg“ in Heidelberg. Ihr Vorgesetzter bittet Sie, eine E-Mail auf Englisch zu verfassen, um die englischsprachigen Kunden des Autohauses zu einer exklusiven Vorstellung eines neuen Modells einzuladen.

Verfassen Sie die E-Mail anhand der Informationen Ihres Vorgesetzten:

- **Noch nie war es einfacher, sein Traumauto zu finden**
- **Stolz ausdrücken, unter den wenigen Autohäusern zu sein, die ausgewählten Kunden eine Vorschau auf den neuen TX7 geben dürfen**
- **Einladung für den 14. April 20.. aussprechen, da er/sie zu unseren langjährigen Kunden gehört**
- **Show fängt um 11 Uhr mit Champagnerempfang und Snacks an**
- **kurze Rede vom Hauptgeschäftsführer, gefolgt von der Enthüllung des TX7**
- **von 12 bis 17 Uhr einmalige Chance auf 30-minütige Probefahrt**
- **Nach diesem spannenden Erlebnis wird der Tag mit einem exklusiven Abendessen ab 18 Uhr abgerundet.**
- **sollen nicht zu lange warten – Plätze sind begrenzt, daher Bitte um frühzeitige Zusage**
- **freundlicher Schlusssatz**

9. Writing an acknowledgement of order

Sie arbeiten bei einem Unternehmen für Badezimmerzubehör und -möbel und Sie sind zuständig für internationale Bestellungen. Gestern haben Sie eine Bestellung von Mr Hamilton von der Firma Indulge Yourself in Brighton erhalten:

Order for bathroom facilities				
Item No.	Quantity	Article No.	Description	Unit Price
1.	30	829/4935	Bath mat “Big Foot”, blue	4.99 €
2.	15	832/0218	Toilet seat, aqua frosted	15.95 €
3.	50	830/1970	Brush holder, stainless steel	12.50 €
4.	80	831/0039	Towel rail, chrome plated	6.30 €
5.	10	830/1385	Shower curtain “Friendly fish”	16.75 €

Schreiben Sie eine Auftragsbestätigung (nur den reinen Brieftext) mit folgendem Inhalt:

- **Bedanken Sie sich für den gestrigen Auftrag über Badausstattungen.**
- **Die ersten vier Artikel werden Anfang nächster Woche ausgeliefert.**
- **Der Auftrag über Duschvorhänge kann leider nicht ausgeführt werden, da sie im Moment nicht auf Lager sind. (Der Hersteller hat mitgeteilt, dass die Lieferzeit bis zu fünf Wochen betragen kann.)**
- **Sie informieren Mr Hamilton, sobald die gewünschten Duschvorhänge wieder verfügbar sind.**
- **Falls er nicht so lange warten kann, bieten Sie ihm ein anderes Modell an, z. B. „Dolphin“ (Artikelnummer 830/1389) mit einem Rabatt von 15 %, bei dem die Lagervorräte aber begrenzt sind. Daher werden die Bestellungen entsprechend des Auftragseingangs bearbeitet und nur, solange der Vorrat reicht.**
- **freundlicher Schlusssatz mit Entschuldigung für Unannehmlichkeiten**

10. Describing departments of a company

You are currently working in the US office of your company. As you are an apprentice in your third year, your American boss would like you to look after two students from Manchester who will do a 3-week internship in the company. He wants you to explain the following six departments to them when they arrive:

- **Personnel**
- **Purchasing**
- **Sales**
- **Dispatch**
- **Accounts**
- **Marketing**

Write down briefly what you are going to say to the students.

11. Writing a letter of complaint

Sie arbeiten in der Einkaufsabteilung einer Elektromarktkette. Als Sie eine Lieferung von Power Supply überprüfen, bemerken Sie einige Fehler.

Schreiben Sie einen Beschwerdebrief an den Lieferanten. Orientieren Sie sich dabei an folgenden Punkten:

- **Dank für die Lieferung vom 28. November**
- **Bedauern ausdrücken, dass die Lieferung Anlass zur Beschwerde gibt**
- **Angabe der Fehler:**
  - **Statt der bestellten zwölf Mini-Stereoanlagen in Blau sind nur sechs in Blau und sechs in Rot geliefert worden.**
  - **Drei Flachbildschirme fehlen, sind aber berechnet worden.**
  - **Anstatt 50 Kartons CD-Rohlinge sind DVD-Rohlinge geliefert worden.**
  - **200 Kataloge sind in Schwarz-Weiß statt in Farbe geliefert worden.**
- **Vorschlag unsererseits:**
  - **Kostenlose Nachlieferung von drei Flachbildschirmen und sechs blauen Mini-Stereoanlagen. Bei Lieferung können die sechs roten abgeholt werden und bleiben bis dahin auf unsere Kosten bei uns eingelagert.**
  - **50 Kartons DVD-Rohlinge würden wir behalten, falls wir einen Nachlass von 15 % auf den Listenpreis bekommen. 50 Kartons CD-Rohlinge bitte innerhalb von einer Woche nachliefern, da sie dringend benötigt werden.**
  - **Die unbrauchbaren 200 Kataloge werden entsorgt.**
- **Zahlung erfolgt erst nach vollständigem Erhalt der Waren**
- **Bitte um Bestätigung**
- **freundlicher Schlusssatz**

12. Writing a quote

Sie arbeiten bei der Druckerei DruckArt in Berlin. Als Sie nach einer Besprechung an Ihren Schreibtisch zurückkommen, finden Sie dort folgende Telefonnotiz:

NOTIZ

Betreff: Anruf von Worldwide Stationary
braucht große Mengen Büromaterial:

3000 Postkarten (verschiedene Motive von London)
1000 einfache Einladungskarten
4000 Geburtstagskarten
(einfacher Schriftzug „Happy Birthday")
1000 Tischkalender, schwarz-weiß, für nächstes Jahr
100 gelbe Briefblöcke A5
Frage, ob wir Erstbestellerrabatt gewähren.
Lieferung zwei Wochen nach Bestelleingang gewünscht.
Dank für schnelles schriftliches Angebot

Schreiben Sie ein Angebot für Worldwide Stationary. Beachten Sie dabei folgende Punkte:

- **Dank für Anfrage und Interesse an Produkten ausdrücken.**
- **Wir bieten:**
  - **3000 Postkarten 0,18 €/St. (aber nur, wenn uns fertige Dateien/Motive zugesandt werden)**
  - **1000 Einladungskarten 0,65 €/St. (ab 750 Stück 0,55 €/St.)**
  - **4000 Geburtstagskarten 0,80 €/St.**
  - **1000 Tischkalender mit Spiralbindung 1,75 €/St.**
  - **100 gelbe Briefblöcke A5 mit je 50 Blättern 1,39 €/St.**
- **Erstbestellerrabatt von 10 % auf den Gesamtbetrag. Ab dem vierten Auftrag über 10.000,00 € gewähren wir einen Mengenrabatt von 15 %.**
- **Lieferung ab Werk innerhalb von zwei Wochen nach Bestellungseingang.**
- **Zahlungsbedingungen: innerhalb von 14 Tagen mit 2 % Skonto, sonst 30 Tage netto**
- **freundlicher Schlusssatz**

13. Writing a reminder

Sie arbeiten bei Holzkiste, einem auf Schränke und Regale spezialisierten Möbelhersteller in München. Bei der Überprüfung der Quartalsabrechnung bemerken Sie, dass ein langjähriger Kunde aus England die letzte Rechnung noch nicht beglichen hat.

Verfassen Sie eine dritte Mahnung an Jackson & Jonson; Ben Miller, 53 Madison Lane, Ipswich, IP4 9HJ, United Kingdom. Achten Sie dabei auf höfliche Formulierung.
Orientieren Sie sich an folgenden Stichpunkten:

- **Auftragsnummer 1234/AD (Regale)**
- **Bezug zu deren Konto herstellen**
- **letztmalig auf unsere Rechnung Nr. 8765 vom 30. August hinweisen, die noch nicht beglichen wurde und nun drei Monate überfällig ist**
- **keine Reaktion auf zweite Mahnung erhalten – weder Zahlung noch Sonstiges**
- **Bedauern zum Ausdruck bringen, da Geschäftsbeziehungen bisher immer gut waren**
- **unsererseits alles nur Mögliche getan, nun soll „Jackson & Jonson" seinen Verpflichtungen sofort nachkommen**
- **zwecks gütlicher Begleichung der Angelegenheit darauf bestehen, dass wir einen Scheck oder eine Banküberweisung innerhalb von fünf Tagen erhalten**
- **falls nicht, müssen wir rechtliche Schritte einleiten**
- **Annahme ausdrücken, dass Vermeidung in gegenseitigem Interesse vorliegt**
- **freundlicher Schlusssatz**

14. Preparing a presentation

You work in the personnel department of a medium-sized software company.
Your head of department asks you to prepare the figures for sick leave time and to give a short presentation in the next meeting. You should also add a short conclusion.

Write down on a separate piece of paper what you are going to say.

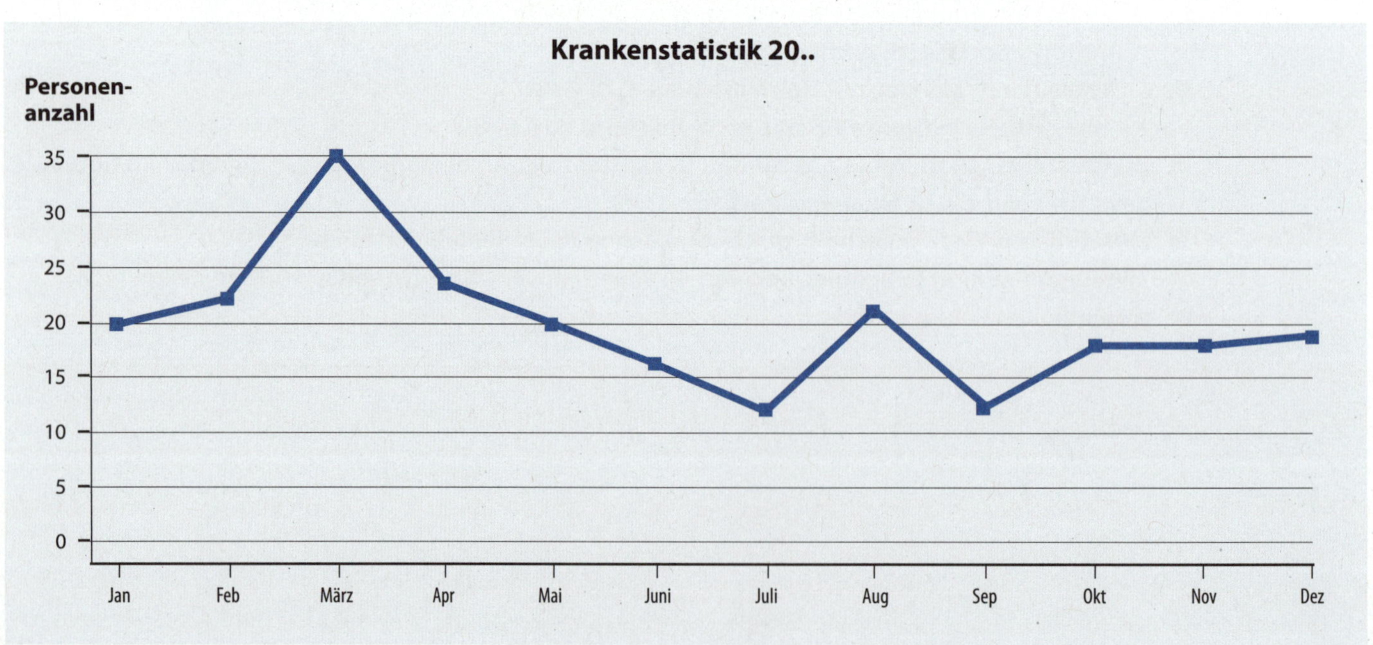

15. Writing a letter of application

You have finished your apprenticeship as an office administrator with Köpke & Sohn GmbH in Frankfurt and you would like to gain some experience abroad. Since you have always wanted to live in the USA, the following Internet job advertisement interests you:

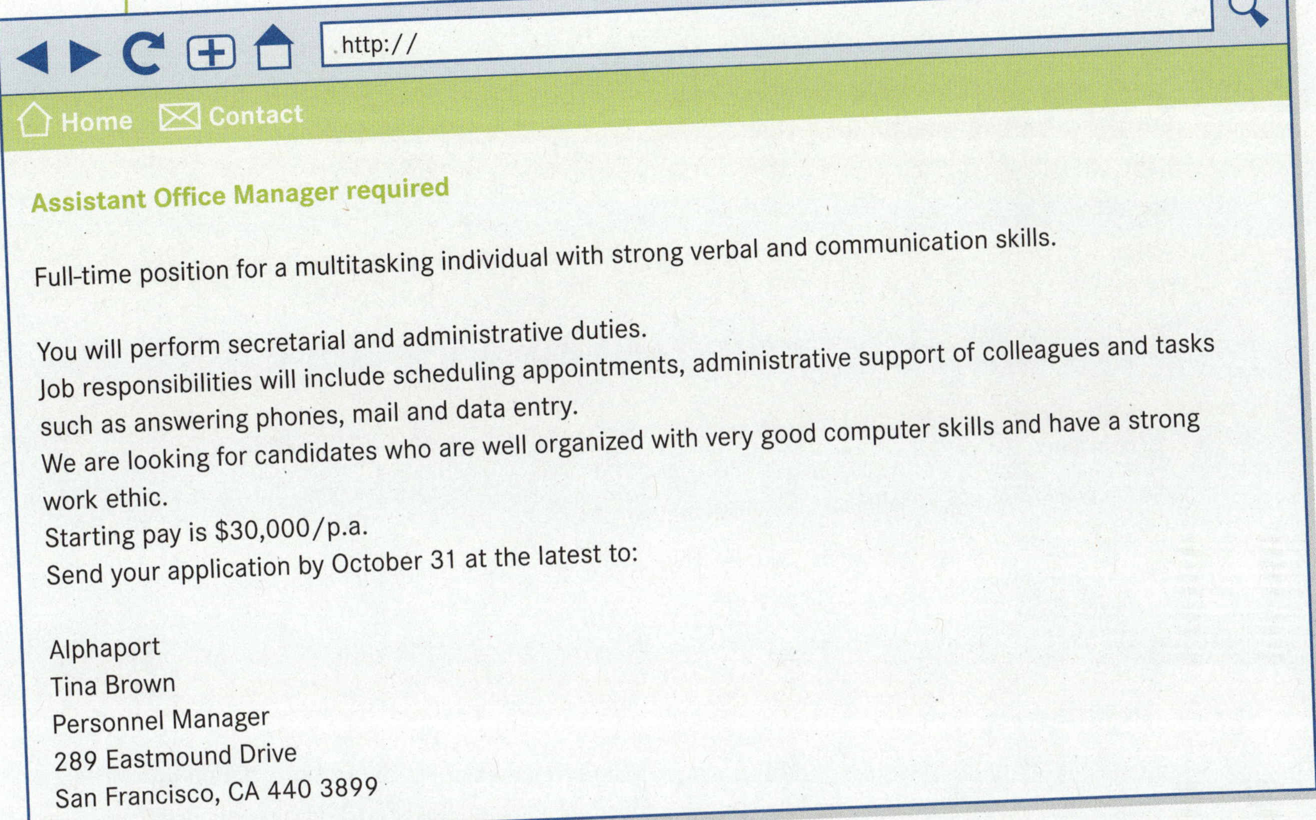

Write a letter of application in English. Include the following information:

- **Bezug auf die Anzeige**
- **Ausbildung in einem renommierten deutschen Unternehmen im Juni erfolgreich abgeschlossen**
- **Suche nach neuer Herausforderung im Ausland in einem anspruchsvollen Unternehmen, das sich schnell entwickelt**
- **Interesse an Stelle äußern**
- **sehr gute Englischkenntnisse in Wort und Schrift**
- **Beziehen Sie sich auf zwei der beschriebenen Verantwortlichkeiten/Aufgaben und drücken Sie Ihre Überzeugung aus, dass Sie aufgrund Ihrer Erfahrung und Fähigkeiten allen Anforderungen entsprechen und deshalb der richtige Kandidat/die richtige Kandidatin sind.**
- **Lebenslauf und Zertifikate über absolvierte PC-Kurse beifügen**
- **freundlicher Schlusssatz**

1. A memo

Sie arbeiten bei der Bacher AG, einem international agierenden Hersteller von Fahr- und Motorrädern.

Da sehr viele Angestellte kein Deutsch sprechen, bittet Ihr Vorgesetzter Sie, die unten stehende Einladung auf Englisch zu verfassen.

MEMO

An: Verkaufsabteilung und alle Abteilungsleiter
Von: Hauptgeschäftsführer
Betreff: Besprechung

Einladung

Die Besprechung bezüglich unserer schlechten Quartalsverkaufszahlen findet am 15. Juli um 10:00 Uhr in Raum 101 statt (1. Stock).

Die Besprechung wird mindestens vier Stunden dauern, ohne die 45-minütige Pause. Mittagessen wird bereitgestellt.

Bitte denken Sie daran, die beigefügten Zahlen mitzubringen.

Falls Sie nicht in der Lage sein sollten, an dieser wichtigen Besprechung teilzunehmen, lassen Sie uns dies bitte umgehend wissen.

2. An email

Sie arbeiten in der Verkaufsabteilung von Der Campingspezialist, einem Unternehmen in Bremen. Sie haben die folgende E-Mail erhalten. Da Sie sich nicht ganz sicher sind, wie Sie antworten sollen, möchten Sie mit Ihrer Vorgesetzten Rücksprache halten.

Aus diesem Grund fassen Sie die wichtigsten Punkte auf Deutsch zusammen, um sie Ihrer Vorgesetzten zeigen zu können.

Hello,
I read on your website that you are a producer of camping equipment.
We are a leading online outdoor specialist based in Newcastle (UK) and interested in

200	2 person tents	article no. 24098	at €39.99 each
300	4 person dome tents	article no. 24763	at €59.99 each
200	mummy bags	article no. 34076	at €14.75 each
400	airbeds	article no. 47809	at €9.99 each

I'd like to enquire about your terms and conditions.
Are all goods delivered by road, plane or ship?
Do you have the above items in stock or how long will it approximately take you to produce any unavailable items?
Will it be possible for you to deliver them within two weeks?
Is it possible to receive a discount on bulk orders? We would appreciate a discount of 20%.
As the goods are required urgently I would be grateful if you could send me confirmation within the next 4 hours.
Thank you for taking the time to answer my questions so quickly.
I look forward to your response.

Jack Stanley
Purchasing Manager
Adventure4you Ltd.
+44 (0)191 261 3498

3. A good offer?

Sie sollen für Ihre Firma 20 neue Kopiermaschinen bestellen. Das beste Angebot entdecken Sie auf der Website eines irischen Großhändlers.

Sie wollen Ihre Kollegen um Rat fragen und fassen deswegen die Eigenschaften des Geräts auf Deutsch zusammen.

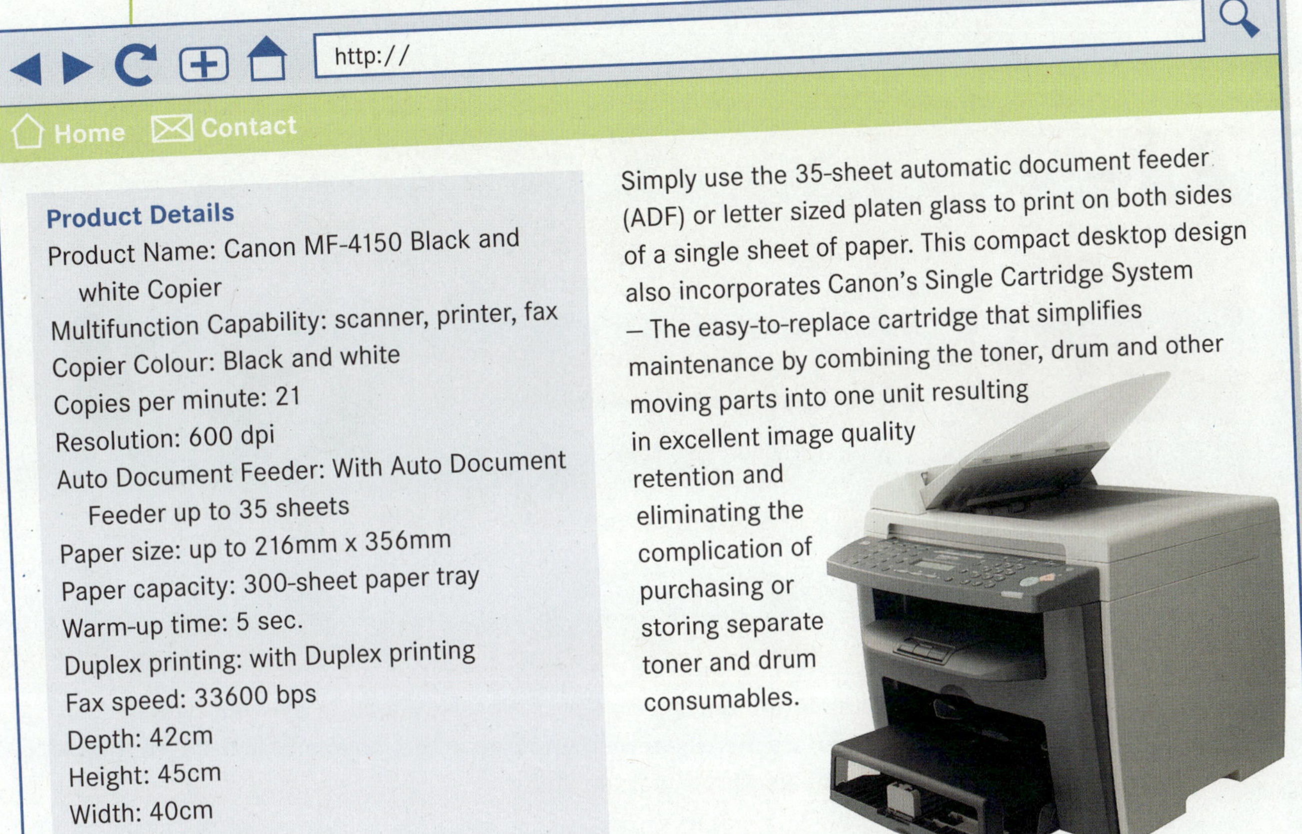

Produktname:	
Multifunktionen:	
Auflösung:	
Aufwärmzeit:	
Kopierfarbe:	
Papierversorgung:	
Papiergröße:	
Kopien pro Minute:	
Automatischer Dokumenteneinzug:	
Beidseitiger Druck:	
Faxgeschwindigkeit:	
Gewicht:	
Breite:	
Tiefe:	
Höhe:	

4. Writing a summary

Sie arbeiten für die Kühlbrecht AG in Darmstadt, einer IT-Firma, mit Zweitsitz in Leeds. Die Firma ist auf der Suche nach einer Werbeagentur für eine neue Marketingstrategie. Sie haben die folgende Anzeige in einer Fachzeitschrift entdeckt.

CreativesFirstCreativesFirstCreativesFirstCreatives

FirstCreatives wurde 2004 von Klaus Gratner und Markus Schnellen gegründet und beschäftigt nun 15 Mitarbeiter.
Wir sind eine innovative Werbeagentur und haben uns mittlerweile zu einer renommierten Agentur im Rhein-Main-Gebiet entwickelt.

Als junges Unternehmen, das kreative Lösungen auf höchstem Standard und in vielen Sprachen für Ihr Unternehmen der IT-Branche anbietet, sind auch wir ständig auf der Suche nach neuen Herausforderungen.

Unsere Ideen werden Sie begeistern, wir sind einzigartig.

FirstCreatives | Grüner Weg 3 | 60320 Frankfurt/Main | +49 69 780348 | info@firstcreatives-wvd.com

FirstCreativesFirstCreativesFirstCreativesFirstCreativesFirstCreatives

Schreiben Sie eine E-Mail an Ihren Kollegen in Leeds. Fassen Sie darin die wichtigsten Informationen in englischer Sprache zusammen und fragen Sie, ob aus Ersparnisgründen eine gemeinsame Werbekampagne gestartet werden sollte.

Von: frankfurt@kuehlbrecht-wvd.de
An: leeds@kuehlbrecht-wvd.co.uk
Betreff: new advertising agency

5. Taking messages

Sie haben den folgenden Artikel entdeckt und wollen die Informationen an einige Kollegen in Großbritannien weitergeben, die oft mit ausländischen Anrufern sprechen.

Fassen Sie die wichtigsten Informationen in englischer Sprache für Ihre Kollegen zusammen.

Nachrichten effektiv entgegennehmen

Einen englischen Anrufer zu verstehen und seine Nachricht korrekt weiterzugeben, ist gar nicht so einfach, besonders wenn Muttersprachler anrufen. Deshalb bekommen viele nur einen Teil wichtiger Informationen mit. Stellen Sie sicher, dass Sie die folgenden Teilinformationen am Ende des Telefonats notiert haben. Hierzu einige Tipps.

1. Namen
Notieren Sie sich den Vor- und Nachnamen. Wenn nötig, bitten Sie den Anrufer, seinen Namen zu buchstabieren.

2. Unternehmen
Finden Sie heraus, ob es ein dienstlicher oder privater Anruf ist und ob Ihr Kollege das Unternehmen kennt.

3. Telefonnummer
Stellen Sie sicher, dass Sie die komplette Telefonnummer notieren mit Orts- und wenn nötig Landesvorwahl. Wiederholen Sie diese noch einmal, um zu prüfen, dass Sie sie richtig gehört haben.

4. Grund des Anrufs
Versuchen Sie den Grund herauszubekommen, warum die Person anruft.

5. Verbleib/Verhalten
Soll zurückgerufen werden oder dient die Nachricht lediglich der Information? Wird der Anrufer sich später noch einmal melden?

6. Uhrzeit des Anrufs
Notieren Sie, wann angerufen wurde. Dies könnte für Ihren Kollegen wichtig sein.

6. Chairing a meeting

Sie sind Angestellter bei BetterPower in Mannheim. Ihr Vorgesetzter, Tim Rolfes, hat bei der Vorbereitung auf ein wichtiges Treffen den folgenden Artikel in einer englischsprachigen Zeitschrift entdeckt.

Verfassen Sie den Artikel in deutscher Sprache für Ihren Vorgesetzten.

Meeting Management

Meetings can be very productive. They can also be a waste of time. Use a "PAT" approach to meetings. A meeting has to have: a Purpose, an Agenda, and a Timeframe. You should be able to define the purpose of the meeting in one or two sentences at most. Set an agenda. Assign a time limit to each agenda item and identify the person responsible to speak. Set a timeframe. At the very least set a start and end time.

Don't Wait
Meetings need to start on time. Don't wait for stragglers to show up. When someone arrives late, don't go back and review what has already been said.

Stay Focused
Every meeting should have a "topic keeper". The topic keeper's job is to interrupt whenever the discussion strays from the topic under discussion.

Keep and send minutes
The minutes should record who attended, what was discussed, any agreements that were reached, and any action items that were assigned. Soon after the meeting, usually within 24 hours, the minutes of the meeting should be distributed.

7. A manual

You are doing an internship in the customer service department of Logshop, a large department store in Bournemouth.
When selling a document shredder to a customer, your colleague discovers that the manual is in German only.

Summarize the main part of the manual in English, so your colleague can pass it on to her customer.

Bedienungsanleitung

Aktenvernichter

Gerät aufsetzen und anschließen

1. Ziehen Sie die Schiene auf die benötigte Länge heraus und setzen Sie den Aktenvernichter auf den Papierkorb. Achten Sie darauf, dass der Aktenvernichter so sitzt, dass er nicht herunterfallen kann.
2. Schieben Sie den Schalter in Position AUTO und stecken Sie den Stecker in eine Steckdose.

Papier zerkleinern

Vorsicht: Entfernen Sie gegebenenfalls Heftklammern, denn sie können das Gerät zerstören.
In der Mitte des Papiereinzugs ist ein Fühler angebracht, der das Gerät einschaltet, wenn Sie Papier einführen. Stecken Sie kleinere Papierstücke deshalb immer in die Mitte des Papiereinzugs hinein.
Sie können bis zu vier Blätter normaler Stärke (je 70 g/m²) auf einmal zerkleinern.
Das Gerät schaltet sich automatisch aus, wenn das Papier durchgelaufen ist.

Papierstau?

Ist das Papier zu dick, wurden zu viele Blätter auf einmal eingeführt oder wurde Papier extrem schräg zugeführt, kann es vorkommen, dass das Papier nicht korrekt zerkleinert wird oder es zu einem Papierstau kommt. Im Falle des Papierstaus schieben Sie den Schalter auf REV (rückwärts) bzw. FWD (vorwärts), um das Papier hin- und herzubewegen und so wieder herauszubekommen.

8. Writing minutes

Sie sind Assistent/-in der Geschäftsführung bei Mainpower GmbH in Magdeburg und zuständig für die Erstellung des Protokolls der monatlichen Verkaufsbesprechung.
Sie haben das Protokoll bereits in deutscher Sprache verfasst.

Schreiben Sie das Protokoll in englischer Sprache. Achten Sie dabei auf angemessene Wortwahl.

Protokoll

Monatliche Verkaufsbesprechung:
22. September 20..

Anwesend:
Christian Altmann, Sandy Baker, Jonathan Beck, Steven Colee, David Grome, Inka Heynemeier, Fritz Leuermann, Robert Marston, Martin Runke, Stephanie Schmitt, Julius Strenke, Mike Swink, Karl Meier (Vorsitzender)

Entschuldigt abwesend:
Susan Williams

Genehmigung:
Das Protokoll der Konferenz vom 4. August wird einstimmig angenommen.

Zu klärende Fragen:
Keine

Verkäufe:
Sandy berichtet, dass die Großbritannien-Verkäufe im Vergleich zu Juni um 4 % gesunken sind, der Juni musste bereits einen Rückgang um 3 % gegenüber den Monaten März bis Mai verzeichnen.
→ Sandy bereitet bis 30. September einen Verkaufsbericht über die letzten sechs Monate vor.

Werbebudget:
Eine Erhöhung des Werbebudgets für das kommende Jahr wird genehmigt. Robert schildert einzelne Probleme mit der „StarTime"-Werbeagentur und empfiehlt eine Strategieänderung. Es wird zugestimmt, dass eine neue Werbeagentur benötigt wird.
→ Steven stellt bis 7. Oktober einen Überblick über die Werbeausgaben bereit.
→ Robert besucht am Freitag, 26. September, die „StarTime"-Werbeagentur, um die Probleme der Werbeaktion zu besprechen.

Verkaufstagung:
Die Hotelkosten werden viel höher als letztes Jahr sein.
Der bevorzugte Tagungssaal ist im März oder April nicht verfügbar.
→ Inka sucht nach Ausweichörtlichkeiten und liefert Preisinformationen bei der nächsten Konferenz.

Sonstiges:
Bert Watson, Leiter der US-Verkäufe, wird am 15. Dezember im Londoner Büro sein.

Nächste Konferenz:
Montag, 13. Oktober 20..

9. A German website

You work for Strategy Counts, a marketing company in London.
The company wants to enter the European market and therefore the website needs to be translated into several languages.

Read the text from the website below and translate it into German.

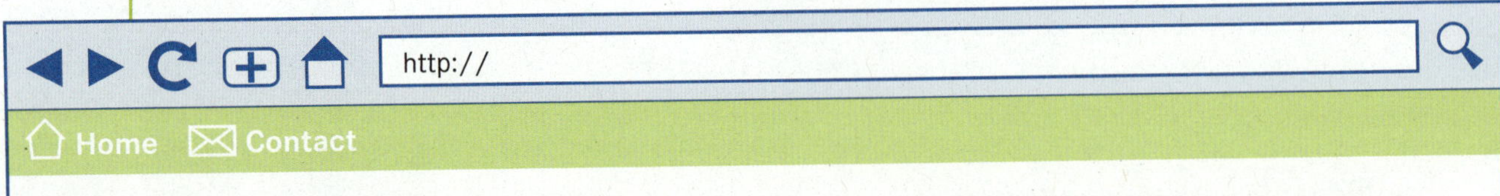

Strategy Counts is the leading marketing firm in London. A lot of our clients are active in the areas finance and insurance. Strategy Counts possesses innovative tools to help you to localise your target group. Strategy Counts plans in real terms. We arrange a highly visible presence in all relevant media and save you money. In Great Britain and now throughout Europe you will benefit from our expertise.
We have been successful since 1987. The formula for success has changed from "Who has the best products or services?" to "Who possesses the best marketing?".
According to this principle, the success of your company is always our focus. Our references and the many, satisfied clients speak for themselves.

Through our demand for high quality standards and experience we have the ability to consult you in a professional and appropriate manner in this sensitive and demanding market segment.

10. Business visits

Sie sind bei der Linea AG in Essen tätig. Ihre Vorgesetzte wird nächste Woche an einer Tagung in New York teilnehmen. Sie bittet Sie um Hilfe, da sie noch nie in den USA war und sich über kulturelle Unterschiede informieren möchte. Sie entdecken diesen Zeitungsartikel.

Fassen Sie die wichtigsten Punkte in deutscher Sprache für Ihre Vorgesetzte zusammen.

Business Visits to the United States

Business visits tend to be extremely punctual. If you arrive late to a business appointment, it will reflect badly on you. So try to arrive on time, or even a little early. If you know that you will be arriving late, you should telephone ahead to let them know of the delay.
If a business meeting takes place over a meal, expect the business discussions to begin after everyone has ordered their meal, sometimes as soon as everyone is seated. Socializing tends to occur after the business is concluded, not before. This is in contrast with the practice in many other countries, where the purpose of the meal is to socialize with and get to know each other before any business is discussed.
Many American companies have women in management positions. So don't be surprised if the person who meets you is a woman, not a man. They are just as competent (if not more so) than their male counterparts. If you feel uncomfortable, focus on the business at hand and ignore the fact that she happens to be a woman. Do not, however, ask personal questions as you might with a male colleague. In particular, do not ask whether she is married or has children. Do not flirt with her, refer to body parts, ask her out on a date, or make suggestive or sexual remarks.
When businessmen or businesswomen meet, they usually introduce themselves by shaking right hands. When you shake hands, don't crush their fingers, but also don't hold their hand too lightly. A firm handshake is best.
Business cards are not normally exchanged upon meeting. If you need a colleague's contact information, it is ok to ask them for their card. It is also ok to offer someone your card. But there is not an elaborate ritual of exchanging cards as in other cultures.

11. Being successful

Sie haben diesen Artikel in einer deutschen Wirtschaftszeitschrift entdeckt und wollen Ihre amerikanischen Kollegen daran teilhaben lassen.

Geben Sie den Text stilistisch und inhaltlich angemessen in englischer Sprache wieder.

Der gute Ton für den beruflichen Erfolg

Beruflicher Erfolg und gutes Benehmen stehen in unmittelbarem Zusammenhang. Wer sich richtig ausdrückt und verhält, punktet nicht nur bei Kunden und Geschäftspartnern, sondern auch bei Kollegen.
Hier ein kleiner Auszug, wie Sie sich stilvoll verhalten.

Begrüßen Sie im Stehen
Nicht nur Männer, auch Frauen stehen auf, um jemanden zu begrüßen. Dabei spielt die Position keine Rolle. Schütteln Sie die Hand und achten Sie auf einen festen Händedruck. Sehen Sie Ihrem Gegenüber dabei in die Augen. Stellen Sie sich mit Ihrem Vor- und Nachnamen vor. Falls Sie einen Titel haben, lassen Sie ihn weg. Wer ihn betont, wirkt eitel.

Gehen Sie voraus
Egal ob Sie einen Kunden vom Firmeneingang zum Besprechungsraum oder einen Geschäftspartner von der Werkshalle zur Kantine begleiten – gehen Sie voraus. Ihr Gast kennt sich bei Ihnen nicht aus.

Schalten Sie das Handy aus
Ihr privates Handy sollte im Büro auf gar keinen Fall klingeln. Stellen Sie es aus oder auf lautlos. Selbst Vibrationsalarm ist in Besprechungen unangebracht. Wer wirklich einen dringenden Anruf erwartet, sollte dies vorher ankündigen. Verlassen Sie den Raum zum Telefonieren.

Halten Sie Ordnung
Strahlen Sie durch die Aufbereitung Ihrer Unterlagen Professionalität aus. Ein Haufen loser Zettel ist in Meetings tabu. Hektisches Durchsuchen kostet Zeit und wirkt unstrukturiert. Nutzen Sie Mappen oder Ordner, um Ihre Unterlagen und Materialien ordentlich einzusortieren.

Kleiden Sie sich korrekt
Herren: Anzüge mit ausgefallenen Schnitten oder auffälligen Farben wirken oft störend. Dunkelblau und Anthrazitgrau passen immer. Bei Hemden und Krawatten dürfen Männer auch zu stärkeren Farben greifen. Aber helle Socken sind nach wie vor verpönt.
Damen: schlicht und elegant ist am besten. Behängen Sie sich nicht mit zu vielen Ketten und Accessoires. Oberteile ohne Ärmel oder mit tiefem Dekolleté sind ebenso unpassend wie sehr kurze Röcke. Damen haben eine größere Farbauswahl als ihre männlichen Kollegen, aber Vorsicht vor knalligen, leuchtenden Farben.

12. Holding presentations

You recently joined Barneys Ltd., an outdoor clothing specialist based in Glasgow, as a sales representative.
You are going to hold a presentation at an international conference in Dublin soon, and you have asked an experienced Scottish colleague for some advice. She sent you an email.

Write a summary of her advice in German so you have it handy for your presentation.

Hello,
I'm glad to help, so here's my advice for the presentation:
Above all know your audience and match what you say to their needs. Prepare your presentation with your audience in mind; that will assure that your audience will be able to follow you. If your presentation doesn't appeal to your audience – no matter how well you have developed your presentation – your presentation will fall on deaf ears.
Also: Know your material thoroughly. Your material needs to be second nature to you. Practice and rehearse your presentation with friends, in front of a mirror, and with colleagues.
Since you will be speaking in a foreign language, it might help you to record yourself and listen a number of times.
Remember that you are an actor when presenting. Make sure that not only your physical appearance is appropriate to the occasion, but also the tone you use is well chosen. If your topic is serious, be solemn.
However, it's always a good idea to begin your presentation with an ice-breaker. Lead the audience through your materials in a calm and relaxed manner. Speak slowly and clearly, and remember to address everyone in the audience – even the person the farthest away from you.
To achieve the above goals follow these tips when giving your presentation:
Speak with conviction. Believe what you are saying and you will persuade your audience.
Do not read from notes. Referring to notes is fine, but do so only briefly.
Maintain eye contact with your audience. Making direct eye contact with individuals will help them feel as if they are participating in your presentation.
Bring handouts. Don't just use a PowerPoint presentation. Provide audience members with handouts of the most important materials so they can keep your most important take always in mind.
Know when to stop. This cannot be underestimated. You need to make your case, but continuing for too long will only ensure that the audience forgets what you have said.

13. Translating for a website

Sie sind bei einem Gepäckhersteller in Rostock angestellt.
Eine Ihrer Produktlinien wird demnächst auf dem britischen Markt eingeführt.

Ihre Vorgesetzte bittet Sie, die Garantie in die englische Sprache zu übertragen.

Travelfun-Produkte werden mit höchstem Qualitätsanspruch sorgfältig gefertigt und unterliegen ständigen Qualitätskontrollen. Sollte dennoch einmal ein Grund zur Beanstandung gegeben sein, leistet Travelfun Gewähr nur unter Maßgabe folgender Richtlinien: Die Garantie deckt ausschließlich Materialfehler und durch mangelnde Verarbeitung verursachte Defekte ab und ist auf den Produktwert beschränkt. Schäden, die auf unsachgemäße Behandlung, oder auf unsachgemäßen Transport durch Dritte zurückzuführen sind, sind durch diese Garantie nicht gedeckt und können von Travelfun nicht anerkannt werden. Die Garantie gilt nur unter Vorlage der ausgefüllten Garantiekarte in Verbindung mit dem zugehörigen Kassenbon. Die 24-monatige Garantiezeit beginnt ab dem gültigen Kaufdatum. Bei gültigen Garantieansprüchen kann statt der Instandsetzung nach Wahl von Travelfun die Ware auch umgetauscht werden. Weitergehende Ersatzansprüche jeglicher Art sind ausgeschlossen. Bei gültigen Garantieansprüchen für Artikel, die nicht mehr im Sortiment von Travelfun geführt werden, behält sich Travelfun das Recht vor, einen vergleichbaren Ersatz zu stellen. Diese Garantie besteht zusätzlich zu den gesetzlichen Rechten.
Da bei Schäden durch Dritte die Herstellergarantie nicht in Kraft tritt, möchten wir Ihnen folgende Empfehlung geben: Überprüfen Sie nach jeder Reise alle Ihre Gepäckstücke sofort in der Gepäckausgabe (ggf. noch vor dem Passieren des Zolls) auf Schäden. Sollten Sie Transportschäden feststellen, reklamieren Sie diese sofort mündlich und schriftlich beim Informationsstand Ihres Beförderers und lassen Sie sich diese Schäden auch schriftlich bestätigen. Bei sofortiger Anmeldung entstandener Schäden beim zuständigen Transporteur können Sie im Allgemeinen mit einer schnellen und großzügigen Regulierung rechnen. Um Ihre Ansprüche erfolgreich geltend zu machen, hilft Ihnen sicherlich auch Ihr freundlicher Fachhändler bei der Erstellung eines Gutachtens/Kostenvoranschlages. Schließen Sie für eine komplette Deckung eine zusätzliche Gepäckversicherung ab.

14. Breaking into the European market

Sie arbeiten bei Largos, einem etablierten Versandhandel, in Hamburg. Largos möchte sich vergrößern und wird demnächst auch europaweit agieren.

Verfassen Sie die Geschäftsbedingungen in englischer Sprache.

Allgemeine Geschäftsbedingungen

1. Rückgaberecht: Sie haben das uneingeschränkte Recht, Ihre bei Largos bestellten Artikel innerhalb von 14 Tagen nach Erhalt der Lieferung ohne Begründung und auf unsere Kosten und Gefahr an die Largos GmbH zurückzusenden.
2. Liefervorbehalt: Lieferungen erfolgen, so lange der Vorrat reicht. Eine Lieferung erfolgt nur innerhalb Europas.
3. Versandkosten: Bei Largos zahlen Sie in der Regel unabhängig vom Bestellwert eine Versandkostenpauschale von 4,95 €. Hierdurch werden die anfallenden Kosten für Porto/Frachten und Verpackung nur teilweise abgedeckt, den Rest übernimmt Largos. In Ausnahmefällen müssen wir eine höhere Pauschale in Rechnung stellen. Diese wird entsprechend ausgewiesen. Sollte aus technischen oder logistischen Gründen eine Versendung in mehreren Etappen erfolgen, berechnen wir die Versandkostenbeteiligung natürlich nur einmal.
4. Eigentumsvorbehalt: Bis zur vollständigen Bezahlung bleibt die Ware Eigentum der Largos GmbH.
5. Zahlung, Fälligkeit, Zahlungsverzug: Die Bezahlung der Waren erfolgt per Bankeinzug oder Kreditkarte. Largos behält sich das Recht vor, im Einzelfall bestimmte Zahlarten auszuschließen. Die Bezahlung durch Senden von Bargeld oder Schecks ist leider nicht möglich. Wir schließen jegliche Haftung bei Verlust aus.
Die Abbuchung bei Zahlung per Kreditkarte erfolgt erst nach Versendung der Ware.
Im Falle eventueller Rücksendungen erfolgt eine Rückerstattung des gezahlten Betrages.
Sollte Ihre Kredit- oder Bankkarte unzureichend gedeckt sein, behalten wir uns das Recht vor, Ihnen die entstandenen Kosten der Zahlungsaufforderung in Rechnung zu stellen.

15. The Autumn Fair

Sie arbeiten in der Einkaufsabteilung von Living Beautiful, einem Großhändler von Deko-Produkten und Geschenken in Düsseldorf.
Ihr Unternehmen möchte mehr internationale Kunden gewinnen. Auf der Suche nach Gelegenheiten dazu haben Sie diese Website entdeckt.

Fassen Sie die wichtigsten Punkte in deutscher Sprache für Ihren Vorgesetzten zusammen.

http://

Home Contact

Welcome to Autumn Fair

Autumn Fair is the UK's biggest and best autumn buying opportunity of the season with major brands, European suppliers and independent designers. Many of them make up a gift and home event that's really worth the trip as you won't find them anywhere else.
Throughout the halls a range of business-building seminars, trend previews, demonstrations and showcases provide even more business insight.

About Autumn Fair

Two main zones, Giving and Living, house 2,000 exhibitors across nine packed product sectors. It's an unmissable chance to pick up articles for the Christmas season, and preview exclusive product launches in the coming year.

Autumn's biggest buying opportunity – three times the size of any other at this time

- Over 500,000 products
- 40,000 new market launches
- Over 2,000 exhibitors
- More than 60,000 visitors from across the world

Your competitors will be here. Make sure you don't miss out.

Product Categories: Art products, bags, gifts, candles, clothing, toiletries, home interiors, fashion accessories, greeting cards, jewellery, toys, promotional gifts

Why Exhibit at Autumn Fair?

Autumn Fair is unquestionably the sales opportunity of the season. Autumn Fair's 60,000+ visitors don't just come to the show to browse - they come to buy. The show's September timing means they're ready to place big orders for the festive season and seek new-season stock.
This autumn, there's nowhere else you should be.

Your only opportunity to meet thousands of high-spending retailers at this time of year.
Make contact with every type of retailer including multiples, independents, online and mail order.
Buyers from all corners of the UK and thousands from overseas.
Benefit from a global marketing campaign targeting a phenomenal database of international retailers.

For further information contact

Autumn Fair Sales
Email: sales@autumnfair-wvd.com

Opening hours

Saturday, 6th September	10am – 5pm
Sunday, 7th September to Wednesday, 10th September	9am – 6pm

1. Making appointments

Role A

You work as an office clerk for Richardson Inc. Your boss, the sales director, Mr Simson, needs an urgent appointment with Mrs Schmidt, the head of purchasing at one of your suppliers. Phone her secretary and use Mr Simson's diary to decide a suitable day and time. Offer alternatives if nothing seems to work out (make a compromise).

Time	Monday	Tuesday	Wednesday	Thursday	Friday
08.00 – 10.00	Staff meeting		Appointment Dr. Miller	Business trip to London	Department meeting
10.00 – 12.00	Staff meeting	Appointment Mrs Pitt		"	Appointment Mr Hoyle
12.00 – 14.00	Lunch Mr Michikato			"	Lunch Mr Hoyle
14.00 – 16.00	Videoconference France	Meeting with new apprentice	Seminar	"	
16.00 – 18.00			Seminar	Return from business trip	

Role B

You work as a secretary for Mrs Schmidt, the head of purchasing at Schmidt & Snyder Computer. You receive a phone call from Richardson Inc. and Mr Simson's secretary who wants to arrange an urgent appointment. Use Mrs Schmidt's diary and try to find a suitable day and time. If it seems difficult, be flexible and make a compromise.

Time	Monday	Tuesday	Wednesday	Thursday	Friday
08.00 – 10.00		Meeting Managing Director	Vienna	Trade fair	
10.00 – 12.00	Meeting production		"	"	
12.00 – 14.00		Business lunch	"		
14.00 – 16.00			"		Leaving for New York
16.00 – 18.00	Staff meeting	Leaving for Vienna	Return from Vienna		

2. The trade fair

Role A

Sie arbeiten als Sekretärin für den Verkaufsleiter der Spielzeuge Händel GmbH. Für die jährliche Spielwarenmesse in London sind einige Vorbereitungen nötig. Hierzu hat Ihnen Ihr Chef eine Notiz hinterlassen. Rufen Sie im Conference Centre an und buchen Sie die gewünschte Ausstattung.

Maria,

bitte nicht vergessen, die zwei Konferenzräume (30 Personen, 15 Personen) zu buchen.
Wir brauchen unbedingt Wireless LAN! Sind die Beamer und die Laptops schon bestätigt?
Zusätzliche Ausstattung, die wir benötigen:
Flip-Charts, Leinwand, vier Tische und 16 Stühle.
Bitte versuchen Sie, dass der Catering-Service uns Kaffee und Getränke nach Bedarf bringen kann.
Es reisen noch zwei Verkäufer mehr mit, bitte prüfen Sie, ob hier noch Einzelzimmer im Conference Centre vorhanden sind.

Danke!
Richard

Role B

You work as an office clerk at the Conference Centre in London. With your team you are responsible for the organisation of the trade fair "Play and Enjoy". You receive a telephone call from Germany. Answer the questions according to your notes and the customer file.

Order NO. 34530KL
Client: Spielzeuge Händel GmbH, Germany
14 single rooms (incl. breakfast)
145m² stand
3 video projectors, 5 laptops

Play and Enjoy Fair
Updated information
Wireless broadband 2 days before fair starts
Hotel rooms available:
1 single, 6 double rooms
Available equipment:
Flipcharts, tables, chairs
Available conference rooms:
2 6 people
1 10 people
2 20 people
1 30 people
Catering service needs exact orders to make sure that required food and drinks will be there on time.

3. Small talk

Role A

You work for Graham Solar Ltd. and have to pick up a visitor at the airport. Introduce yourself and ask the visitor about the flight, the trip and about other typical topics which are suitable for small talk.
Be prepared to answer questions about the area, attractions and so on.

Role B

You have just arrived in Germany. After getting through customs and collecting your luggage you are greeted by a representative of the company you're visiting.
Introduce yourself and answer questions about your flight, your trip and other typical topics which are suitable for small talk.
Ask questions about the area, attractions etc.

4. The apprenticeship

You work for SAHEBI Inc., a manufacturer of mobile phones. Next week some of the trainees from your subsidiary in the USA will be visiting. Since you have just completed your apprenticeship, the head of human resources asks you to present something about the apprenticeship in Germany (keywords: school vs. company, exams, departments and activities in an office/a company ...).

Bemerkung: Als Einzelprüfung geeignet, bei zwei Prüflingen abwechselnde und ergänzende Stellungnahme und Ergänzungen.

5. An enquiry about office equipment

Mithilfe der vorgegebenen Struktur führen Sie ein Telefongespräch.

Rolle A: Lieferant

A: Sie nehmen den Anruf entgegen (Name, Firma, Begrüßung).

A: Sie haben den Namen nicht genau verstanden und bitten darum, ihn zu buchstabieren.

A: Sie haben nun alles verstanden und fragen nach, welcher Artikel angefragt werden soll.

A: Sie erwidern, dass Sie kurz im System überprüfen müssen, ob die Stühle verfügbar sind. ...
15 Stühle können kurzfristig geliefert werden, die anderen in zwei Wochen.

A: Sie nennen einen Stückpreis von 178,00 €. Bei dieser Menge gibt es einen Rabatt von 5 %. Sie wollen wissen, ob der Kunde die Stühle bestellen will.

A: Skonto ist möglich, Lieferung erfolgt ab Werk, die Kosten für die komplette Lieferung betragen 256,00 €.

A: Sie bestätigen die Bestellung, fassen noch einmal zusammen und sagen zu, einen Katalog zuzusenden. Dann weisen Sie noch darauf hin, dass im kommenden Monat die Firma auf der Büromöbelmesse vertreten ist.

A: Sie verabschieden sich.

Rolle B: Kunde

B: Sie melden sich mit Namen und Firma und sagen, dass Sie eine telefonische Anfrage haben.

B: Sie buchstabieren Ihren Namen.

B: Sie benötigen für Ihren neuen Konferenzraum noch 20 Bürostühle. Im Internet haben Sie sich für das Modell EM9000 entschieden. Sie möchten wissen, ob diese Stühle auch kurzfristig lieferbar sind.

B: Sie erklären, dass das ausreichend ist, und erkundigen sich nach dem aktuellen Stückpreis und einem möglichen Mengenrabatt.

B: Bevor Sie bestellen, möchten Sie gerne noch die Liefer- und Zahlungsbedingungen klären. Sie erkundigen sich nach möglichem Skonto bei Zahlung innerhalb von einer Woche.

B: Sie bestellen die Stühle zu den angegebenen Bedingungen. Zusätzlich bitten Sie um die Zusendung eines aktuellen Katalogs mit Preisliste.

B: Sie danken für den Hinweis und verabschieden sich.

6. The job interview

Role A

Sie haben sich um die folgende Stelle beworben:

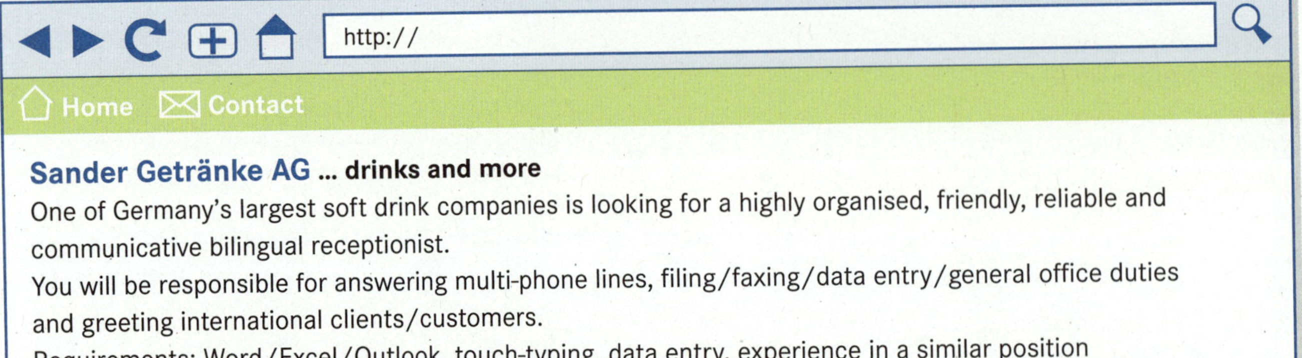

Sie erhielten eine Einladung zum Vorstellungsgespräch. Da Sie viel mit englischsprachigen Kollegen und Kunden zu tun haben werden, wird das Vorstellungsgespräch in Englisch stattfinden.
Zur Vorbereitung auf das Gespräch haben Sie sich bei Freunden, in Büchern und im Internet darüber informiert, mit welchen Fragen Sie rechnen müssen. Dabei ist folgende Liste entstanden:

- **kurze eigene Vorstellung, bisherige Erfahrungen**
- **warum man sich gerade für diesen Job bei dieser Firma interessiert**
- **Stärken/Schwächen – Was hebt einen von anderen Bewerbern ab?**
- **Wie geht man mit viel Arbeit und Stress um?**
- **Arbeit im Team**
- **Fragen stellen, z. B. nach der Größe der Abteilung, Möglichkeiten für Fortbildung usw.**

Role B

Sie sind die Personalleiterin/der Personalleiter der Firma Sander Getränke AG und suchen für folgende Stelle eine(n) neue(n) Mitarbeiter(in):

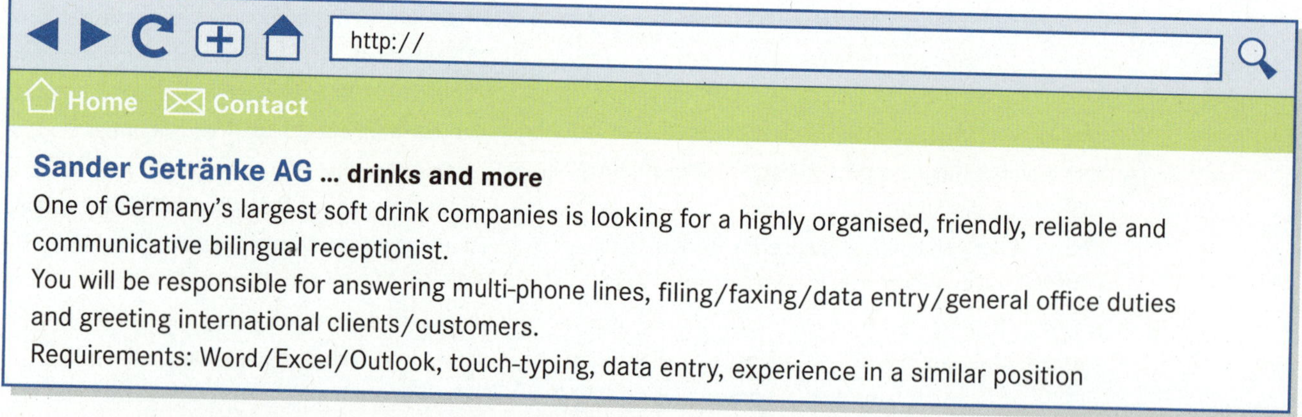

Heute führen Sie mit dem ersten infrage kommenden Bewerber ein Vorstellungsgespräch, das Sie auf Englisch führen, um gleich die sprachliche Eignung festzustellen.
Folgende Stichworte sollen Ihnen bei Fragen im Gespräch helfen:

- **Erfahrungen des Bewerbers**
- **Warum will der Bewerber zu unserer Firma?**
- **Stärken/Schwächen – Warum sollten wir uns für Sie entscheiden?**
- **Wie sieht sich der Bewerber bei Stress und in Bezug auf Teamarbeit?**
- **Der Bewerber hat Gelegenheit, Fragen zur Firma (Fortbildung, Abteilung, in der er/sie eingesetzt wird ...) zu stellen.**

7. Giving advice

As part of your training as an office clerk, you gain quite a bit of experience in many areas.
Talk about your experiences on the following topics and give advice what to do and what to avoid.
Which problems can occur?

a) telephoning
b) job applications/job interviews

Bemerkung: Als Einzelprüfung geeignet, bei zwei Prüflingen abwechselnde und ergänzende Stellungnahme und Ergänzungen.

8. Complaint about a delivery

Role A

You work in the purchasing department of Mastermetal Ltd. You have just received a delivery of spare parts which is not up to standard.
You take the order confirmation and the note from the warehouse to phone the supplier to find out what happened and how to proceed. Since the spare parts are really important for production, the matter is quite urgent.

Metalflex Inc.

Order 2008-673-KL

Qty	product	price/unit
120	XST 14	714,38
100	LTMP 8	1839,56
120	GHJ 6000	345,78

Mastermetal Ltd.

Goods in
Order 2008-673-KL

110	XST 14	714,38
90	LTMP 8	1839,56
120	MJH 7000	345,78

Notes:
Packaging: 4 boxes
1 damaged, 10 XST 14 broken, MJH 7000 obviously not on our order, only 90 LTMP 8

Role B

You work for Metalflex Inc., a manufacturer of spare parts. You receive a call from one of your best customers because a delivery was not up to standard. Use the order confirmation and the note from the dispatch department and try to explain why things went wrong. Offer compensation and/or replacement.

Mastermetal Ltd.

Your order 2008-673-KL

Qty	product	price/unit
110	XST 14	714,38
100	LTMP 8	1839,56
120	MJH 7000 (identical in construction with GHJ 6000)	345,78

Metalflex Inc.

dispatch
Order: 2008-673-KL

110	XST 14	714,38
90	LTMP 8	1839,56
120	MJH 7000 (identical in construction with GHJ 6000)	345,78

Packaging: 4 boxes, no damage
Forwarding agent: Quality Transport
Note: 10 pieces of LTMP 8 were broken so we sent only 90 pieces.

9. The advertising campaign

Ihre Firma Cottondreams plant eine neue Werbekampagne für das neue Produkt „YOUR SHIRT“, ein Shirt, das man mit seinem eigenen Design bestellen kann. Sie arbeiten in der Marketingabteilung der Firma. Jeder Mitarbeiter des Projektteams „YOUR SHIRT“ ist zu einem Treffen eingeladen, um Ideen für Werbemaßnahmen und Strategien zu sammeln. Die besten Ideen sollen dann von den beiden Projektmanagern ausgearbeitet und weiter verfolgt werden.
Da die Firma ihren Hauptsitz in den USA hat und viele internationale Mitarbeiter in den Abteilungen arbeiten, ist die Firmensprache hauptsächlich Englisch. Daher wird auch das Treffen in Englisch abgehalten.

A

Sie sind davon überzeugt, dass das Produkt so gut ist, dass man auf alle Fälle Radio- und Fernsehwerbung machen sollte. Die hohen Kosten könnten durch den durch die Medien hergestellten Bekanntheitsgrad und somit einen hohen Absatz gut wieder hereingeholt werden.
Machen Sie konkrete Vorschläge, welche Radio- und Fernsehsender für Sie infrage kämen, zu welchen Uhrzeiten und eventuell in welchem Sendeumfeld (Kinderprogramm, Horrorfilm, Nachrichten, ...) die Werbespots gezeigt/ausgestrahlt werden sollten.
Stellen Sie die Vorzüge der Medien Fernsehen und Radio im Vergleich zu anderen Medien, die eingesetzt werden könnten, klar heraus.
Nutzen Sie Ausdrücke und Redewendungen, die Zustimmung und (teilweise) Ablehnung ausdrücken.

B

Sie vertreten den traditionelleren und günstigeren Ansatz, zunächst regional durch Anzeigen in Zeitungen den Markt zu testen. Weiterhin wollen Sie durch gezielte Werbeaktionen auf regionalen Märkten und Festen die Kunden auf das neue Produkt aufmerksam machen. Durch Verteilung von Prospekten und dem Aushängen von Postern sowie durch Gewinnspiele soll dieses Konzept ergänzt werden.
Machen Sie konkrete Vorschläge, in welcher Art von Zeitungen Sie Anzeigen schalten wollen und wie häufig. Wo sollten Prospekte verteilt und Poster aufgehängt werden? Welche Art von Gewinnspiel könnte es sein?
Stellen Sie die Vorzüge des Mediums Zeitung im Vergleich zu anderen Medien, die eingesetzt werden könnten, klar heraus.
Nutzen Sie Ausdrücke und Redewendungen, die Zustimmung und (teilweise) Ablehnung ausdrücken.

C

Sie wollen den Erfolg des Shirts durch Werbung im Internet erreichen. Weiterhin denken Sie an Sponsoring.
Begründen Sie, wie die Werbung konkret aussehen soll und wie sie erfolgen soll.
Erklären Sie, welche Art von Sponsoring Sie sich vorstellen und welchen Erfolg Sie sich versprechen.
Stellen Sie die Vorzüge dieser Werbearten gegenüber anderen deutlich heraus.
Nutzen Sie Ausdrücke und Redewendungen, die Zustimmung und (teilweise) Ablehnung ausdrücken.

Möglich als Einzel-/Partner- und Gruppenprüfung.
Einzelprüfung: nur Rollenkarte A
Partnerprüfung: Rollenkarten A + B
Gruppenprüfung: Rollenkarten A + B + C

Bei einer Partner- oder Gruppenprüfung würde der Prüfer die Rolle des Vorsitzenden des Treffens übernehmen und die Sitzung leiten.

Rezeption	Hörverständnis	KMK-Stufe I (A2, Waystage)

Sie sind bei der Traber GmbH angestellt, einem international tätigen Unternehmen mit Hauptsitz in Deutschland.
Thomas Scott, der Verkaufsleiter für Großbritannien und Irland, hat eine Bitte an Sie.

Vervollständigen Sie das Formular.

NOTIZ

AB-Nachricht für: *Thomas Scott*

Abwesend von: **bis:**

Wünscht Weiterleiten der Gespräche: ☐ ja ☐ nein

Alternativ erreichbar unter:

Weitergabe der Alternativnummer an Anrufer: ☐ ja ☐ nein ☐ nur an bestimmte

Erwartet wichtige Anrufe von:

Traber GmbH

Rezeption	Leseverständnis	KMK-Stufe I (A2, Waystage)

Nachdem Sie die Anrufbeantworter-Nachricht für Herrn Scott aufgenommen haben, möchten Sie seinen E-Mail-Abwesenheitsassistenten einrichten.
Sie finden im Internet einige interessante Artikel zu dem Thema und möchten die Informationen an Ihre deutschen Kollegen weitergeben.

Vervollständigen Sie dazu die Tabelle auf Deutsch.

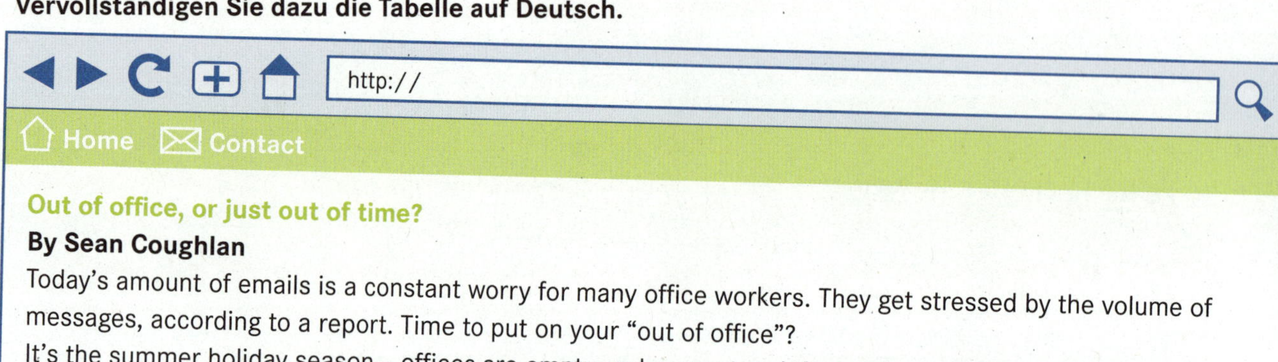

Out of office, or just out of time?

By Sean Coughlan

Today's amount of emails is a constant worry for many office workers. They get stressed by the volume of messages, according to a report. Time to put on your "out of office"?
It's the summer holiday season – offices are empty and computers left sleeping and even if you try to email someone, all too often you'll get an "out of office" message.
But are they really away? This is a conversation overheard between two workers: "I thought you were away on holiday? I got an out of office."
"No, I put that up a couple of days before, so no one expects me to answer their emails."
People are using the out of office like answering machines to screen their calls.

Turn off e-mail and do some work

By Jane Wakefield

Intel has become the latest in an increasingly long line of companies to launch a so-called 'no email day'. On Fridays, 150 of its engineers revert to more old-fashioned means of communication.
In actual fact email isn't strictly forbidden but engineers are encouraged to talk to each other face to face or pick up the phone rather than rely on email.
According to US research firm The Radicati Group, individual workers sent an average of 37 emails a day in 2006 with predictions this will rise to 47 by the end of this year.
When email behaviour was tracked it was found that many were checking their inbox as often as 30 to 40 times per hour.

Text 1: 1. Gründe, warum Arbeitnehmer ihre „out of office"-Nachricht einrichten (bei E-Mails und Telefonen)	______ ______
2. Was soll am „no email day" nicht passieren?	______ ______
Text 2: 3. Wozu werden die Ingenieure bei Intel ermutigt, anstatt eine E-Mail zu schreiben?	______ ______
4. Wie viele E-Mails wurden 2006 täglich im Durchschnitt von einem einzelnen Angestellten versandt?	______ ______
5. Was machen viele Arbeitnehmer 30-mal bis 40-mal in der Stunde?	______ ______

Produktion	KMK-Stufe I (A2, Waystage)

Verfassen Sie die Abwesenheits-E-Mail in englischer Sprache für Thomas Scott. Die E-Mail sollte folgende Punkte enthalten:

- **Anrede**
- **Dank für Nachricht**
- **Grund der Abwesenheit (Geschäftsreise nach Holland) und Rückkehr ins Büro am Montag, 26. April angeben**
- **Antwort wird so bald wie möglich nach Rückkehr erfolgen**
- **Falls es um eine dringende Lieferung geht, bitte Assistentin Kirsten Müller kontaktieren, +49 161 883672323 oder an k.mueller@traber-wvd.com**
- **Allgemeine Produktnachfragen bitte an Loreley Gibson, l.gibson@traber-wvd.com, richten**
- **Grußformel**

Von: t.scott@traber-wvd.com
An: ____________________
Betreff: ____________________

____
____
____
____
____
____
____
____
____
____
____
____
____
____
____
____
____

Thomas Scott
Head of Sales
E-Mail: t.scott@traber-wvd.com

Mediation KMK-Stufe I (A2, Waystage)

Den folgenden Artikel über Abwesenheits-Nachrichten haben Sie in einer Zeitschrift entdeckt.

Übertragen Sie ihn für eine Kollegin ins Deutsche.

How to write out-of-office replies

Style: It's best to adopt a formal tone. Begin with a neutral and formal greeting, such as "Dear Sir or Madam". Do not begin the email with "Ladies and gentlemen", as this is used only for formal speeches, never for emails or letters.

Politeness: Always thank the sender. It's more polite to write "Thank you for your email/message" than just to say "Thanks".

Important details: You don't have to explain why you are not in the office, unless you think it is relevant. State clearly when you will return. Write the date in full and include the day of the week so that there are no misunderstandings.

Positive points: Say what you *will* do, not what you won't do. Write "I will answer your email as soon as I can when I return". Inform the recipient if the email has been forwarded.

Alternatives: List the contact details of the people who will be able to deal with any urgent messages in your absence. Include their names, positions, email addresses, and telephone numbers including the country code.

Signature: Add your signature with your company's full name and address in case someone would like to send you something by post.

Mündliche Prüfung	KMK-Stufe I (A2, Waystage)

Sie sind Kirsten Müller, die Sekretärin von Thomas Scott. Nach seiner Rückkehr von der Geschäftsreise in Holland führen Sie folgendes Gespräch mit ihm:

Sie begrüßen Herrn Scott und erkundigen sich, wie seine Reise war.

Sie fragen nach interessanten neuen Produkten.

Sie erwähnen zwei wichtige Anfragen für Gartenausrüstung, die heute noch beantwortet werden müssen.

Sie verneinen und verabschieden sich, da Sie selbst noch eine Besprechung haben.

Sie sind Thomas Scott. Nach der Rückkehr von der Geschäftsreise führen Sie folgendes Gespräch mit Ihrer Sekretärin, Frau Müller:

Sie begrüßen Frau Müller und sagen, dass die Reise sehr erfolgreich war.

Sie erwidern, dass Sie einige neue Blumen und Pflanzen bestellt haben, und fragen, ob etwas Wichtiges in der Firma passiert ist.

Sie versichern, dass Sie sich gleich darum kümmern werden, und fragen, ob Sie heute noch einen Termin haben.

Sie danken für die Hilfe und verabschieden sich.

Rezeption	Hörverständnis	KMK-Stufe II (B1, Threshold)

Sie erhalten einen Anruf von Duggins Ltd. aus Großbritannien. Leider gab es Probleme bei der letzten Lieferung.

Füllen Sie das Beschwerdeformular aus.

Beschwerdeformular

Datum: ____________________

Kunde (Firma und Name): ____________________

Bestellnummer: ____________________

Referenznummer: ____________________

Problem mit Bestellung:

☐ noch nicht angekommen ☐ falsche Ware ☐ beschädigte Ware

Details: ____________________

____

____

Problembehandlung: ____________________

____

____

Rezeption	Leseverständnis	KMK-Stufe II (B1, Threshold)

In letzter Zeit haben sich immer häufiger Kunden wegen Lieferproblemen beschwert. Auch mit einer Lieferung für Ihren größten Kunden gab es bereits Schwierigkeiten.
Ihr Vorgesetzter bittet Sie, einige Informationen für einen Workshop über den Umgang mit Beschwerden zu sammeln. Bei Ihrer Recherche stoßen Sie auf den folgenden Zeitungsartikel.

Machen Sie sich Notizen, indem Sie die Fragen auf Deutsch beantworten und die Übersicht auf S. 66 vervollständigen.

Why & How to Deal With Customer Complaints

It is a fact of business life that not all customers will be happy, even in the finest run businesses, problems, mistakes, or even bad luck can cause people to be dissatisfied with your products or service: hence 'customer complaints'.
When people are unhappy, they will often complain. Many businesses tend to try and ignore complaints, or pass them off as irrelevant, however, if dealt with well, they can actually provide your business with a strong advantage. The following is a look at some of the ways in which your customers might complain, and how you can deal with them, and turn an unhappy customer into a satisfied one.

Types of Customer Complaints

(I) Letters

Letters are a very common form of complaint; they are generally seen as the most official way of complaining. This means that most customers will only use a letter of complaint where they feel there is a serious dissatisfaction, and where the business has a separate address for complaints or head office.
Letters have an advantage to your business, as they allow you time to look at a problem, solve it, and reply to the customer; hopefully ensuring they are satisfied enough to remain a customer.

(II) Spoken Word to Employees

The most common form of complaint, particularly in retail businesses; is face to face with an employee (usually the front line staff). This could take the form of a passing word or gesture, and can be for small or large problems. Typical comments include things such as: "This is not the first time...", "I can't believe that ..." or even a 'tut' noise in a sentence. They are generally informal complaints or comments, only occasionally do they turn into full scale complaints.
Although there is no official complaint in most cases, spoken word comments can provide information on the everyday problems that customers are experiencing, and provide an opportunity for your employees to solve these problems, both for these customers, and for future ones.

(III) Phone Calls

These are another common form of complaint, generally used for informal minor complaints, but can also be used by a highly dissatisfied customer who does not wish to write. The frequency of phone complaints generally depends on how much your business uses the phone; a call centre will receive many more complaints than a basic office line.
Phone complaints allow you to look into a problem, but do not usually give you as much time to solve it as a letter or email.

(IV) Email

Emails are similar to letters; however they tend to describe smaller problems that are expected to be solved in a much quicker time. The number of email complaints you receive will depend mostly on how widely you use email, and whether there is a specific enquiry or complaints email address.

1. **Wodurch entstehen Beschwerden von Kunden?**

2. **Wozu tendieren viele Unternehmen im Bezug auf Beschwerden und was sollten sie stattdessen tun?**

3. **Welche Vorteile haben Beschwerden in Briefform?**

Vervollständigen Sie die Übersicht:

Art der Beschwerde	Häufigkeit	Voraussetzung
Brief		
direkte Ansprache an den Verkäufer		
Telefongespräch		
E-Mail		

Mediation	KMK-Stufe II (B1, Threshold)

Sie erhalten das angekündigte Fax von Duggins Ltd.

Fassen Sie es auf Deutsch zusammen, damit Sie das weitere Vorgehen mit Ihrem Vorgesetzten besprechen können.

Fax Message

Duggins Ltd
432 Main Street
Bournemouth
BH1 2LW
Tel.: +44 10239-420
Fax: +44 10239-421

To: Lampenfieber GmbH Hamburg, Mr Schmidt
Ref: order no. DG 4829
Date: 5th July 20..
Fax no.: +49 4049765 0

Dear Mr Schmidt

As I explained on the phone, unfortunately, the last delivery has given reason for complaint again.
Three crates out of ten were badly damaged. They had been dropped by the forwarding agent when he unloaded the goods.
Half of the lamps and the bulb sockets were completely broken and therefore unsaleable.

This incident is especially sad as this was the second time in a row and several lamps were reserved for important customers. Since we promised to have them in stock by the end of this week we now assume that we will lose at least some of those faithful customers.
In order to avoid this loss we insist on an immediate delivery free of charge of 30 lamps, order no. K3P754. Additionally, we would appreciate if you engaged a different transport agent.
If you fail to fulfil these conditions we must ask for compensation to cover our losses.
Please let us know what you want us to do with the damaged goods.
We are looking forward to your prompt reply.

Yours sincerely

David Duggins

Produktion	KMK-Stufe II (B1, Threshold)

Nachdem Sie mit Ihrem Vorgesetzten und dem Leiter der Versandabteilung Rücksprache gehalten haben, beschließen Sie, der Spedition ein Fax zu senden.

Verfassen Sie das Fax in englischer Sprache. Folgende Punkte sollten darin enthalten sein:

- **Berichten Sie von dem Anruf von heute Morgen und geben Sie die Bestellnummer an.**
- **Schreiben Sie, dass sich nun schon zum wiederholten Mal Kunden über schlecht ausgeführte Lieferungen beschwert hätten.**
- **Versichern Sie, dass die Waren in bestem Zustand Ihr Unternehmen verlassen haben, das Problem daher in der Spedition aufgetreten ist.**
- **Beziehen Sie sich auf die bisherige gute Zusammenarbeit und drücken Sie Ihre Hoffnung aus, dass in Zukunft keine Probleme mehr auftreten werden.**
- **Bitten Sie um Zustellung der Ersatzlieferung am nächsten Tag.**
- **Sie hoffen, dass nunmehr die Lieferung zur vollen Zufriedenheit ausgeführt wird.**

Fax Message

Lampenfieber GmbH
Bremer Str. 99
20034 Hamburg
Tel.: +49 40 49764-0
Fax: +49 40 49765-0

To:	Shirley Jenkins, Roadster Logistics	**Date:**	5th July 20..
Ref:	Order no. ____________	**Fax no.:**	+44 11750871

Mündliche Prüfung	KMK-Stufe II (B1, Threshold)

A

Sie sind Shirley Jenkins von der Spedition Roadster Logistics und erhalten einen Anruf von Toni Schmidt von der Lampenfieber GmbH, in dem es um die Kosten des entstandenen Schadens geht. Folgende Aspekte sollten im Gespräch vorkommen:

- Begrüßung
- Ihre Versicherung kann nur ca. die Hälfte des Schadens ersetzen.
- Eigene Firma übernimmt den Rest, da die Lampenfieber GmbH ein guter Kunde ist.
- Erneute Entschuldigung für die Unannehmlichkeiten, Verständnis signalisieren, Betonung, dass man die Lampenfieber GmbH als Kunden halten möchte.
- Schaden war eine Ausnahme, da er nicht von firmeneigenen Mitarbeitern verursacht wurde.
- bei Terminvorschlägen Alternativen geben

A

B

Sie sind Toni Schmidt von der Lampenfieber GmbH. Sie rufen Shirley Jenkins von der Spedition Roadster Logistics wegen der schadhaften Lieferung an. Folgende Aspekte sollten im Gespräch vorkommen:

- Bezahlt die Versicherung von Roadster den Schaden?
- Eigene Kosten für Ersatzlieferung waren sehr hoch, voller Ersatz der Kosten ist ein Muss!
- Kurzfristige wichtige Ersatzlieferung über einen anderen Spediteur abgewickelt
- Deutliche Enttäuschung über erneute schadhafte Lieferung
- Ist mittlerweile der eigentliche Grund des Schadens bekannt?
- Vereinbarung eines Treffens, an dem neue Vereinbarungen über die Zusammenarbeit verabschiedet werden sollen

B

Rezeption	Hörverständnis	KMK-Stufe III (B2, Vantage)

Your company is expecting visitors from Sweden. You welcome them at reception and guide them to the meeting room.

Listen to the conversation and answer the questions.

1. **Which company do the visitors work for?**

2. **How did they travel to Germany and how long did it take?**

3. **Why are the visitors from Sweden interested in a cooperation?**

4. **How old is the Swedish company they work for?**

5. **How many employees does the Swedish company have and where are they based?**

6. **How long is the meeting going to be?**

7. **Where are the visitors staying?**

Rezeption	Leseverständnis	KMK-Stufe III (B2, Vantage)

Since you want to start business relations with a Swedish company you try to get some information about the Swedish business culture.

Make notes by answering the questions on the following page.

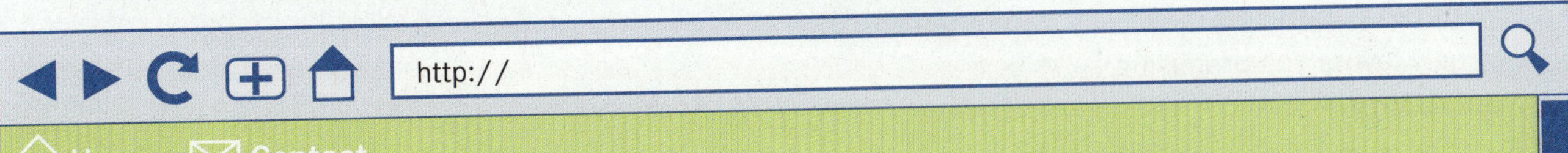

Home Contact

Overview of Business Culture in Sweden

Management Style

Swedish management is based on the idea that the individual is both willing and able to do a good job. A Swedish manager tends to think of himself as a coach rather than a commander, and he often delegates tasks and authority to his staff. In Swedish organizations, employees of all levels have the freedom to make decisions and solve unexpected problems without asking superiors for permission.

A good manager, according to Swedish standards, is a person who takes advantage of the natural creativity and motivation of his staff. He should lead the employees not through his power or formal position, but through the principles of cooperation and agreement. Being a good listener is considered to be another important quality. In discussions with his staff, a professional manager should use reason and base his views on facts. Getting emotional when discussing a problem is considered rather inappropriate.

Power Distance

The power distance in Swedish companies is among the smallest in the world, according to a study of 40 countries in 1984. "Power distance" can be defined as "the extent to which people in a hierarchical situation feel they can and should control the behavior of others, and the extent to which those others are conditioned by reflexes of obedience". In Swedish companies, the concept of power distance is largely replaced by personal responsibility.

Personal status is of relatively small importance in Swedish business life. Managers only rarely give signals of their own status and employees normally don't feel inferior to them. An executive is most of all considered to be a specialist in managing companies and he is therefore not socially superior to a specialist in any other field. In this respect, Sweden seems to differ from many other countries. A further sign of the non-hierarchic (or, better, modestly hierarchic) Swedish company structure is that Swedes normally use their first names at work.

Organizations

Swedish organizations are probably less rigid than many of their foreign counterparts. Swedes try to solve problems in an informal and pragmatic way, even if it means bypassing one or more layers of executives. In most cases, managers do not feel threatened by this practise, the general idea being that decisions are made in order to achieve a result and not to demonstrate your own position. The same attitude explains the vivid exchange of information in Swedish companies. If people know what is going on, the argument goes, they will feel more involved, and therefore more motivated for work.

Swedish companies usually have a flat and team-oriented structure with few management levels. The result is a simple and direct decision-making process. Matrix organizations are common, since Swedish employees often report to more than one manager.

The Approach to Risks

Swedish executives are generally more willing to take risks than their colleagues in other countries. An international study showed that Sweden had the lowest "uncertainty avoidance index" by far among the countries compared, while Japan had the highest. To generalize this result, one could perhaps say that Swedish managers are not so anxious to do the 'right' thing as long as they do their best.

In countries where managers show a high uncertainty avoidance, employees are often promoted according to seniority. In Sweden, on the other hand, actual work performance tends to be of greater importance. As a result, young men and women are frequently seen in leading positions.

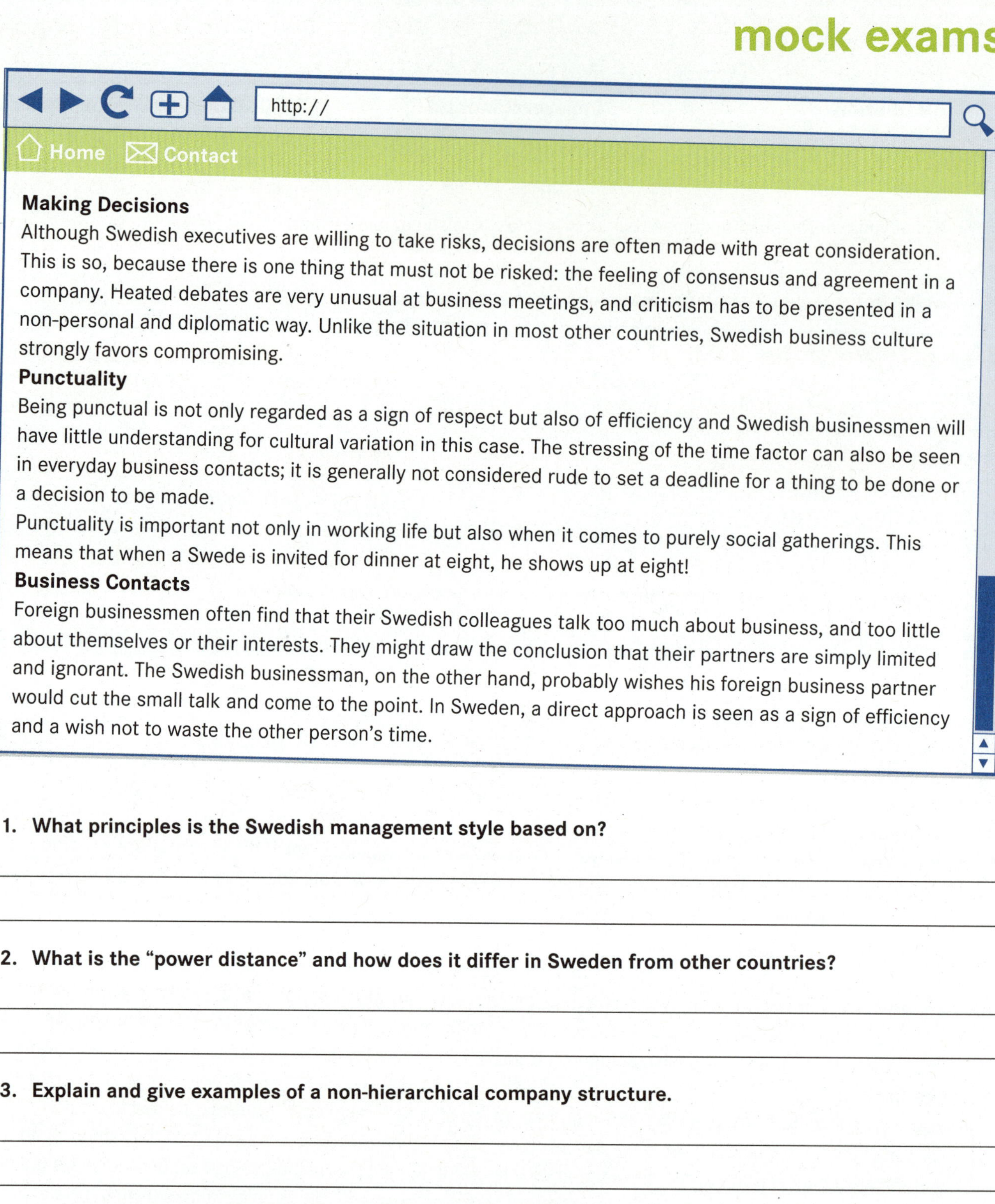

Making Decisions

Although Swedish executives are willing to take risks, decisions are often made with great consideration. This is so, because there is one thing that must not be risked: the feeling of consensus and agreement in a company. Heated debates are very unusual at business meetings, and criticism has to be presented in a non-personal and diplomatic way. Unlike the situation in most other countries, Swedish business culture strongly favors compromising.

Punctuality

Being punctual is not only regarded as a sign of respect but also of efficiency and Swedish businessmen will have little understanding for cultural variation in this case. The stressing of the time factor can also be seen in everyday business contacts; it is generally not considered rude to set a deadline for a thing to be done or a decision to be made.

Punctuality is important not only in working life but also when it comes to purely social gatherings. This means that when a Swede is invited for dinner at eight, he shows up at eight!

Business Contacts

Foreign businessmen often find that their Swedish colleagues talk too much about business, and too little about themselves or their interests. They might draw the conclusion that their partners are simply limited and ignorant. The Swedish businessman, on the other hand, probably wishes his foreign business partner would cut the small talk and come to the point. In Sweden, a direct approach is seen as a sign of efficiency and a wish not to waste the other person's time.

1. **What principles is the Swedish management style based on?**

____

____

2. **What is the "power distance" and how does it differ in Sweden from other countries?**

____

____

3. **Explain and give examples of a non-hierarchical company structure.**

____

____

4. **Describe Swedish employees approach to problem-solving.**

____

____

5. **How do attitudes to promotion differ between Sweden and other countries?**

____

____

6. **What should you avoid in dealings with Swedish counterparts?**

____

____

Produktion	KMK-Stufe III (B2, Vantage)

Die deutsche Firma, für die Sie arbeiten, möchte in den schwedischen Markt eintreten und sieht die Prodata B.V., Stockholm, als potenziellen Kunden.

Verfassen Sie eine Anfrage an Prodata in englischer Sprache. Die folgenden Punkte sollten enthalten sein:

- **Grußformel**
- **Bezug auf Internetauftritt (Hersteller von Hightech-Produkten wie PCs, Laptops, Druckern, Bildschirmen, Fotoapparaten etc.)**
- **Vorstellung des eigenen Unternehmens (großer Hersteller von qualitativ hochwertigen Mikrochips und Leiterplatinen [circuit boards] und führend in der Zuliefererindustrie)**
- **Bekannt für Lösungen auf dem neuesten Stand der Technik**
- **Produkte sind zuverlässig und langlebig**
- **Kunden in Deutschland, Frankreich, Italien und Spanien sind vorhanden, nun Eintritt in schwedischen Markt für dieses Jahr vorgesehen**
- **Suche nach schwedischen Kunden, die beste Verarbeitung, hergestellt in Europa, suchen**
- **Deshalb ist PRODATA richtiger Kunde zum Aufbau von Geschäftsbeziehungen**
- **Katalog beifügen für weitere Informationen zu unserem Unternehmen und unseren Produkten**
- **Einzelheiten zu Preisen, Lieferungs- und Zahlungsbedingungen würden wir gerne in einem persönlichen Gespräch in München verhandeln**
- **Schlusssatz**

MIKRONET AG

Sendlinger Str. 127
80331 München
Germany
Tel. +49 89 1234567
Fax. +49 89 1234500

PRODATA B.V.
Ringvägen 79
11529 Stockholm
Sweden

18th February 20..

Mediation KMK-Stufe III (B2, Vantage)

Sie haben im Internet einige Informationen über PRODATA B.V. entdeckt. Die Informationen sind auf Deutsch.

Fassen Sie die wichtigsten Informationen in englischer Sprache zusammen. Achten Sie dabei auf folgende Punkte:

- **Art des Unternehmens und wo tätig**
- **Ziele**
- **Unternehmerisches Denken**
- **Was für Privat- und Geschäftskunden angeboten wird**
- **Fakten**
- **Umweltaspekte/Engagement**

PRODATA B.V. ist ein Technologieunternehmen, das in mehr als 170 Ländern weltweit tätig ist. Wir untersuchen kontinuierlich, wie Technologien und Services für Menschen neue Möglichkeiten bieten können, um die täglichen Herausforderungen zu meistern und ihre Potenziale, Wünsche und Träume zu verwirklichen. PRODATA B.V. nutzt frisches Denken und innovative Ideen, um den Umgang der Kunden mit Technologien einfacher, wertvoller und vertrauenswürdiger zu gestalten. Unser Ziel ist es, das Leben und die Arbeit unserer Kunden, vom Privatkunden bis hin zum größten Unternehmen, mithilfe unserer Technologieprodukte und Services zu verbessern.

Kein anderes Unternehmen bietet ein so umfassendes Produktportfolio wie PRODATA B.V. Dazu gehören auch Produkte und Lösungen im Infrastruktur- und Geschäftsbereich. Für Privatkunden halten wir ein großes Produkt- und Dienstleistungsangebot bereit, das Digitalfotografie, Digital Entertainment sowie die Drucker- und PC-Nutzung zu Hause vereinfacht. Dieses umfangreiche Portfolio hilft uns, unseren Kunden die Technologielösungen anzubieten, die speziell auf ihre Bedürfnisse abgestimmt sind.

Fakten in Kürze

- PRODATA B.V. wurde 1975 gegründet.
- Der Firmensitz befindet sich in Stockholm (Schweden).
- Vorstandsvorsitzender ist Kalle Bergstrom.

PRODATA B.V. gehört zu den weltweit größten IT-Unternehmen und erzielte im Geschäftsjahr 2007 einen Umsatz von 104,3 Milliarden €.

Engagement

PRODATA B.V. möchte einen wirtschaftlichen, intellektuellen und gesellschaftlichen Beitrag für jeden Ort, an dem wir tätig sind, leisten. Schwerpunkte unseres Engagements sind die Reduzierung von Elektronikschrott, die Anhebung der Standards in der globalen Beschaffungskette von PRODATA B.V. und der Ausbau des Zugangs zur Informationstechnologie.

Mündliche Prüfung KMK-Stufe III (B2, Vantage)

Finally the arrangements for the meeting with PRODATA B.V. in Munich have been made and the day of the meeting has come.
The task of the following meeting is to negotiate prices as well as conditions of payment and delivery. Moreover some product details and possible adjustments need to be discussed.

A

You are the Purchasing Manager at PRODATA B.V. and you arrive at MIKRONET's Munich office where you are welcomed by the Sales Manager.
What you should do during the meeting:

- ask questions about MIKRONET.
- express interest in their products
- make clear what kind of MIKRONET's products are of interest
- mention possible adjustments you need
- ask about possible trial orders
- mention the quantities you will probably order and ask for prices and discounts
- ask about the conditions of payment
- make sure you can order CIF

If you think the meeting went well, come to an agreement.

A

B

You are the Sales Manager at MIKRONET and welcome the guest from Sweden to your company.
What you should do during the meeting:

- be prepared to answer questions about your company
- outline some of your products
- mention how flexible you are in your production and the importance of customer satisfaction
- ask about possible future orders
- answer questions about prices and discounts
- be prepared to answer questions about conditions of payment and delivery (ex works is your standard)
- mention the upcoming trade fair where your company will be present, invite the Purchasing Manager to visit you there and try to make an appointment with him/her.

B

Rezeption Hörverstehen

1. Taking a message

Susanne Müller: Bürobedarf Heinemeier.
Tony Miller: Hi, this is Tony Miller. I'd like to speak to Anne Wilke, please.
Susanne Müller: I'm sorry, Ms Wilke isn't at her desk at the moment. Can I take a message?
Tony Miller: Oh. OK, well I'm ringing about the order we placed ...
Susanne Müller: OK, could you tell me the name of your company?
Tony Miller: Sorry, of course, it's "Office to go". And my name's Tony Miller.
Susanne Müller: Thanks, Mr Miller. And the address, please?
Tony Miller: It's two five five Roman Road, London, E two zero AA.
Susanne Müller: Right, and could you give me your phone number so that Ms Wilke can call you back?
Tony Miller: Sure. It's zero zero four four two zero eight five six nine five one.
Susanne Müller: OK, and you're ringing about an order, you said ...?
Tony Miller: That's right. We placed an order yesterday and we'd like to add a few more items to it.
Susanne Müller: Right, do you have an order reference number?
Tony Miller: Sure ... let me see, BD four five six QW one two.
Susanne Müller: OK. I'll let Ms Wilke know you called and she'll get back to you as soon as possible.
Tony Miller: Thank you.
Susanne Müller: Thanks for calling, Mr Miller. Goodbye.

2. Rooms available

Glenda: Edinburgh Thistle Hotel, my name's Glenda. How can I help you?
Arne Weiher: Hello, I'm Arne Weiher. I'd like to book some rooms from the twenty-third to the twenty-sixth of July.
Glenda: Sure, let me just see what we have available. How many rooms would you like?
Arne Weiher: Two doubles and four singles, please.
Glenda: And that would be for three nights?
Arne Weiher: Yes, that's right.
Glenda: OK. I'm afraid we don't have all those rooms available. We only have one double and two singles.
Arne Weiher: OK, erm, well I think that's better than nothing ... What are the rooms like? Are they ensuite?
Glenda: Yes, all our rooms are ensuite. The rooms are also air-conditioned and have tea and coffee-making facilities as well as a mini-bar.
Arne Weiher: Is internet access available?
Glenda: Yes, there's a modem point in each room.
Arne Weiher: OK. That sounds good. How much are the rooms?
Glenda: The singles are a hundred and thirty-five pounds per night and the double is ninety-eight pounds per person per night.
Arne Weiher: OK. I'd like to book the double and the two single rooms then. Could you tell me where I might be able to book the other rooms I need?
Glenda: You could try Edinburgh Park Hotel. The number's zero one two five four five seven eight nine six three.
Arne Weiher: Thank you.
Glenda: Right, so let me take down your details ...

3. Office Supplies

John: Good morning, Office Supplies Total, John speaking.
Mary: Hi John. This is Mary from DFG Logistics.
John: Hello Mary, what can I do for you today?
Mary: Well, we need to stock up on some stationery ...
John: OK, let me just get your account up on the screen: OK, here we are, DFG Logistics.
Mary: OK, there's quite a lot this month actually ... we need nine boxes of inkjet paper, A four, not laser. Oh, make it ten, instead. And fourteen packets of labels, the light blue ones.
John: Right, labels. Paper, do you need any coloured paper? There are some new colours out: sunshine yellow, apple green and salmon pink. We've got a special offer on them this month, five for the price of four.
Mary: No ... I don't think so but I'll double-check. I'll phone you later, if we do need some. Now, let me see ... We need lots of envelopes, too. threetousand white ones, A four with windows.
John: Right, no problem. There are five hundred in a packet, so that's six of those ...
Mary: ... and a thousand brown envelopes.
John: A four, too?
Mary: No, sorry. A thousand brown envelopes, A five, plain.
John: OK, at two hundred a packet that makes five packets. So, anything else?
Mary: Could you put in a selection of ballpoint pens, blue and black, I don't think we need the red ones.
John: I'll put in three boxes of assorted ones. There are eighty in a box. Will that be enough?
Mary: Yes, I think so. Can you deliver tomorrow morning, please?
John: No problem. Is nine o'clock OK?
Mary: Fine, John. Thanks. Bye.
John: Bye.

4. Preparing for a meeting

Mary-Ellen: Hello?
Gerda: Hi Mary-Ellen. This is Gerda from the Bonn office.
Mary-Ellen: Hi Gerda. How are you?
Gerda: I'm fine, thanks. How are you?
Mary-Ellen: Fine, thank you. I guess you're calling about Tyler, Peter and Danny coming over ...
Gerda: Yes, that's right. I'd like to set up the conference room for them so I wanted to ask you a few things.
Mary-Ellen: Go right ahead, Gerda.
Gerda: Right ... so I know they are going to do a presentation. What will they need for that?
Mary-Ellen: Well they'll bring their laptops but they'll need a projector, a whiteboard or flip-chart, if you've got one, and pens and so on, nothing special ...
Gerda: OK.
Mary-Ellen: Oh sorry, I just remembered they want to use visual aids for the presentation so they'll need some USB sticks from last year's collection, a few computer mice, mouse mats and USB hubs.
Gerda: Right ... well I hope I'll manage to find all that. Also, we would like to take them out to a Greek restaurant for lunch and then have coffee and cake in the afternoon.
Mary-Ellen: Greek sounds fine. Coffee and cake? Well I'm not sure. Tyler's very healthy, you know. He only drinks water and herbal tea and he definitely doesn't eat cake ...
Gerda: OK, I'll get some herbal tea then ...
Mary-Ellen: That'd be good and Danny's allergic to nuts, so please be careful with the cakes.
Gerda: Right, I'll let the caterer know. OK, Mary-Ellen, thank you for your help.
Mary-Ellen: No problem. I only wish I could come over. I'd love to see Bonn ...

5. Problems with a delivery

Frank Neumeir: Möbel Meister, Neumeir. Was kann ich für Sie tun?
Ted Hoskins: Hello. My name's Ted Hoskins. I'm phoning about an order I placed online a few weeks ago.
Frank Neumeir: OK, Mr Hoskins. Can you confirm your address, please?
Ted Hoskins: Certainly. It's thirty-four Station Road, Guildford, GU one three WR, Great Britain.
Frank Neumeir: OK, and do you have a reference number for the order?
Ted Hoskins: Yes, it's QWE one four five two.
Frank Neumeir: So, Mr Hoskins. What seems to be the problem?
Ted Hoskins: Well, I ordered a wardrobe and a chest of drawers on your website about three weeks ago. It said delivery should take about ten days but I only received the order yesterday.
Frank Neumeir: Oh, I'm sorry to hear that.
Ted Hoskins: The problem is you delivered the wrong things! I ordered the wardrobe "Lava" in birch and the chest of drawers "Volt" in dark blue ...
Frank Neumeir: And what did you get?
Ted Hoskins: Well, I got a wardrobe, "Alfa" in pine, and I didn't get the chest of drawers at all. I got a chair, "Ching" it's called!
Frank Neumeir: Oh dear. Right, on the system it says that one wardrobe, "Lava" in birch, and one chest of drawers, "Volt" in dark blue, were delivered yesterday afternoon ... .
Ted Hoskins: I don't care what it says on your system. I got the wrong order!
Frank Neumeir: It's possible that our delivery company has mixed up your order with another customer's. Unfortunately I won't be able to get in touch with anyone there today, so I'll ring them first thing in the morning.
Ted Hoskins: OK and then you'll let me know straight away what you intend to do?
Frank Neumeir: Of course, I ...
Ted Hoskins: If I don't hear from you by tomorrow afternoon, I'll be in touch with my solicitor!
Frank Neumeir: No need for that, Mr Hoskins. I'll give you a call tomorrow. Now, if you'll just confirm your phone number.
Ted Hoskins: It's zero zero four four one one five four seven three two one four.
Frank Neumeir: OK, Mr Hoskins, I'll be in touch tomorrow.
Ted Hoskins: You'd better be. Goodbye.
Frank Neumeir: Goodbye.

6. Telephone query

Michaela Hannhaus: SDR Kommunikation. Guten Tag.
Joanne Keele: Yes, hello. Can I speak to Mrs Thomas, please? This is Joanne Keele from Morehouse Communications, UK. I'm the credit controller there.
Michaela Hannhaus: I'm sorry, but Mrs Thomas is out of the office today. Can I help?
Joanne Keele: Yes, I'm phoning about an unpaid invoice.
Michaela Hannhaus: Can I have your supplier number, please?
Joanne Keele: Our supplier number is MHCOM three one two four nine seven.
Michaela Hannhaus: OK. So that's Morehouse Communications, Warehouse twenty-three, Milton Park, Didcot, OX fourteen three DR, UK.
Joanne Keele: Yes, that's correct.
Michaela Hannhaus: Now, which invoice are you referring to?

Joanne Keele: Our invoice number thirteen A.
Michaela Hannhaus: Thirteen A. I'm afraid I can't find that on the system. When did you send it to us?
Joanne Keele: Well, we sent it four weeks ago on the first of May.
Michaela Hannhaus: I'm sorry but it looks as if we didn't receive it, otherwise it would be on the system. Can you confirm the order details, please?
Joanne Keele: Well, the order was for thirty of our Executive phones. The order number was GLO one three five four four.
Michaela Hannhaus: OK. Let me just check that. Order GLO one three five four four. The order was delivered on the fourth of May to our warehouse in Bremen.
Joanne Keele: That's right. But as I was saying, we still haven't been paid!
Michaela Hannhaus: Again, I apologise. How much is outstanding?
Joanne Keele: Four hundred and eighty-nine pounds seventy-two.
Michaela Hannhaus: OK. I'll tell you what I'll do. I'll initiate that payment by bank transfer immediately. It should reach you within the next five days. In the meantime, please could you resend or fax through the invoice for our records? I think the original must have got lost in the post.
Joanne Keele: OK. Fine, I'll do that. I was sure it must have been something like that. You don't usually pay late.
Michaela Hannhaus: No, we try not to. Thanks for calling, Mrs Keele.
Joanne Keele: OK. Thanks. Bye.
Michaela Hannhaus: Bye.

7. Stock control

Mike Dalton: Hello, JB Electricals UK, Mike Dalton speaking.
Nicole Bergmann: Hi Mike. It's Nicole Bergmann from Purchasing in Hagen.
Mike Dalton: Oh, hi Nicole. How are you doing?
Nicole Bergmann: I'm fine, thanks. How are you?
Mike Dalton: Great. Thanks. So, what can I do for you?
Nicole Bergmann: Well, I'm phoning about stock levels. I was just wanting to double-check that you've got everything you need in the run-up to Christmas. According to this week's report, stock levels are quite good ...
Mike Dalton: Good idea. Let me see. Right here we go ...
Nicole Bergmann: OK, so let's start with TV sets.
Mike Dalton: Yeah, OK. We still need to stock up on a few items actually.
Nicole Bergmann: Right. What do you need?
Mike Dalton: Digital LCD TVs: Model Vision sixty-five, about two hundred and fifty of those, and Model thirty-two LD, I'd say a hundred of those. They're really expensive so we're not expecting to sell that many of them.
Nicole Bergmann: How much are you selling them for?
Mike Dalton: One thousand four hundred and ninety-nine pounds for Vision sixty-five and one thousand eight hundred pounds for thirty-two LD.
Nicole Bergmann: OK, so do you need any more TVs?
Mike Dalton: No, we've got enough stock of the other models. We need to get a few more stereos though. They're selling really well at the moment.
Nicole Bergmann: Right. Which ones?
Mike Dalton: The DanceMaster five thousand, retailing at two hundred and ninety-five pounds each, three hundred in orange and three hundred in black. We also need the HiFi two zero three four PowerStation. It's our bestseller at only ninety-nine pounds, so one thousand of those.
Nicole Bergmann: OK. Anything else?
Mike Dalton: Yeah the iWalk station, model number W seven five two. Five hundred of those. We'll be selling them for four hundred and fifty pounds each.
Nicole Bergmann: Not bad! OK, I'll place a purchase order for those items. I'll have to check the lead times with our supplier in Korea, but I think we should have the stock with you by the fifteenth of October.
Mike Dalton: Great! One thing. Instead of sending the items to the Basingstoke warehouse, could you freight them to our Reading warehouse, attention Les Hooper?
Nicole Bergmann: Will do, Mike.
Mike Dalton: Excellent. Thanks Nicole. Take care. Bye.
Nicole Bergmann: Bye.

8. Email for you

David: Welcome everybody to today's seminar about effective emailing. My name's David Green and I'm from the HR team. I'm responsible for all in-house training.

Firstly, a major problem is receiving a large number of emails every day. Dealing with all these emails can take up a large proportion of someone's day and can lead to people forgetting their other work priorities.

So, how should you deal with too many emails? Ideally, set a time twice a day to read and write emails. Give yourself a time limit for dealing with emails and try to stick to it. Set up labelling options, which will help you manage your emails more efficiently. Review the sender and the subject matter of the email. If the email isn't relevant for you and your job, delete it. Delete junk mail immediately. Unsubscribe from any irrelevant mass mailings and ask to be taken off unnecessary distribution lists.

Be aware of the company's email protocol and make sure that you abide by the rules. Don't write an email or send attachments about anything that's personal, sexist, racist or rude. In some cases, a careless remark can cost someone their job. Don't forget that although emails tend to be more informal than other types of business communication, you shouldn't write anything in them that you wouldn't be happy with someone printing out and presenting to others, so make sure that the tone is professional at all times and that your message cannot be misunderstood. There's also a danger to overuse email. Think twice before writing an email and ask yourself if it's really necessary and the best way of getting your message to others.
So, I think those are the main points that I'd like to cover. Does anyone have any questions before I go into more detail?

9. Travel itinerary

Fiona West: Oyster Travel, Fiona speaking.
Sandra Biegemann: Hello, this is Sandra Biegemann from FitWorld Plc. I'd like to book some flights for my boss, Diane Kramer.
Fiona West: Certainly. So, what are the details?
Sandra Biegemann: Well, we need a flight from London Heathrow to New York on the twelfth of September.
Fiona West: OK, let me see what we've got. Right, there are flights leaving at ten twenty-five, fifteen forty and eighteen o-five.
Sandra Biegemann: Mmh, what time does the fifteen fourty land?
Fiona West: At eighteen fifteen local time ... The eighteen o-five gets in at twenty thirty-five local time.
Sandra Biegemann: I think the fifteen forty would be best.
Fiona West: OK, so that's the twelfth of September at fifteen forty from London Heathrow arriving in New York JFK at eighteen fifteen.
Sandra Biegemann: Great. Could you also book a hotel in New York for two nights from the twelfth of September?
Fiona West: I'll just see what's available. OK, how about the "Queen's hotel" in Manhattan? It's very central and room rates are average for New York.
Sandra Biegemann: OK, that sounds good as Diane has quite a few appointments in Manhattan the next day. She's at Central Gym at four thirty pm and with Betty Jones from the "New York Fitness Co." from five thirty. Right, the next day, the fourteenth of September, Diane will need a flight from New York to Chicago.
Fiona West: OK. There's a flight at one fifty pm from New York's LaGuardia airport arriving in Chicago at three thirty pm.
Sandra Biegemann: No, I'm afraid that's no good. Diane would need an earlier flight as she's got an appointment with Phil Marks at eleven am.
Fiona West: OK; leaving LaGuardia at seven am, arriving in Chicago at nine thirty-five am.
Sandra Biegemann: Yes, that's perfect. Please could you also book her a room at the Grand Mid-Western hotel? We have special business rates with them.
Fiona West: Will do.
Sandra Biegemann: Diane will then be going from Chicago to Denver on the fifteenth of September, leaving Chicago in the morning.
Fiona West: OK, I can offer you a flight at eight twenty-five am arriving in Denver at nine fifty-five.
Sandra Biegemann: Excellent. Could you also book a hotel in Denver for one night only?
Fiona West: Well, there's the "Park Hotel". It's a few miles out of town, is that OK?
Sandra Biegemann: Yes, that should be alright. And last but not least! On the sixteenth of September Diane will be wanting a flight back to London Heathrow.
Fiona West: Let's see. She can leave at sixteen fifty, arriving in London at eleven fifteen the next day.
Sandra Biegemann: That's fine. Could you fax me through the flight details and prices?
Fiona West: Yes, will do. Was that all?
Sandra Biegemann: Yes, thanks, Fiona. Bye!
Fiona West: Bye, Sandra!

10. Finding a conference room

James Monkton: Hello, Armada Hotel. James speaking. How can I help you?
Susanne Fanger: Hello, I'm Susanne Fanger and I'm calling from Power Plastics in Germany. We're wanting to host a conference in London and would like to find out more about your conference facilities.
James Monkton: Well, we have one fully equipped meeting room for a total of sixteen people. The room has all the usual equipment that you'd expect, plus a forty-two inch plasma screen and a DVD player, etc.
Susanne Fanger: And how much would it cost to hire the room?
James Monkton: Well, it costs four hundred and eighty pounds per day.
Susanne Fanger: And what about catering?
James Monkton: We do all the catering ourselves. There's tea, coffee and biscuits on arrival, at mid-morning and mid-afternoon as well as sandwiches and soft drinks at lunchtime. Wine can be provided, but costs extra.
Susanne Fanger: Please can you confirm the hotel's location?
James Monkton: We're located in central London, five minutes' walk from Paddington Station.
Susanne Fanger: Thanks for your help. I'll be in touch again if I want to make a booking.
James Monkton: A pleasure. Bye!

Sally Horton: Hello, GIL Conference Services.

Susanne Fanger: Yes, hello. I'm looking to book a conference room end of July for sixteen people. Please could you tell me about your facilities?

Sally Horton: Yes, certainly. What would you like to know?

Susanne Fanger: Where are you based?

Sally Horton: Our conference rooms are located in West London, five hundred yards from Shepherd's Bush tube station.

Susanne Fanger: Which size conference rooms do you have?

Sally Horton: I'd recommend our boardroom style meeting room for you. It has a twenty person capacity and can be hired by the half-day or day, depending on what you'd prefer.

Susanne Fanger: So, what would the cost be per day?

Sally Horton: Well, the basic rate would be six hundred and fifty pounds. The price includes all catering: welcome drinks plus tea, coffee, water and biscuits throughout the day and a hot buffet lunch.

Susanne Fanger: What equipment is available in the meeting room?

Sally Horton: Standard equipment consists of an overhead projector, screen, flip chart, note pads, pens, laptop docking stations, etc. State of the art video-conferencing facilities and wireless internet are also included, at no extra cost. If you're interested in making a reservation, we offer a ten percent discount if you book a minimum of two months ahead.

Susanne Fanger: That sounds good, though I'll have to think about it. Can I call you back later?

Sally Horton: Yes, certainly. I'm in the office for the rest of the day.

Susanne Fanger: Thank you. Goodbye.

Sally Horton: Goodbye.

11. Preparations for the trade fair

Thomas and Nigel: Hi Martin!

Martin: Hi Thomas, hi Nigel.

Nigel: First off, thanks Martin for volunteering to help out on the stand this year. It's going to be hard work but I'm sure the experience of attending your first motor show will make it worthwhile.

Thomas: So, here's some background information for you, Martin. The trade fair's the biggest motor show in North America with some two thousand exhibitors. Every year it's in a different city and this year it's going to be in Baltimore from the first through the eighth April.

Martin: OK, so when should I arrive in Baltimore?

Thomas: Well, although we send the exhibits to the venue some two weeks before the fair, we only start setting up the stand two days before the fair starts. So if you can join us for the twenty-ninth of March, that would be great. This year, as you know, we have an extra large stand which means that a larger number of exhibits than usual will need to be checked and unpacked. There'll be five of us from the Denver office, myself and Thomas included, but we'll really need your help to keep us on track.

Martin: So can you tell me a bit more about the stand?

Nigel: Well, it's a hundred and twenty square metres and is, I think, in a prime location. Our competitors are going to be jealous!

Thomas: Yeah, it's on the ground floor of the main exhibitor's hall and is right next to the conference rooms. Potentially there'll be a lot of traffic throughout the day.

Nigel: What we need to do now though is to think about how we can get those people to visit our stand rather than just walking by. Do you have any ideas, Martin?

Martin: Well, how about having refreshments on the stand? We all know that people get hungry and thirsty if they're in and out of meetings all day, so I'm sure that if we offered refreshments, we'd be able to attract visitors to stop by our stand.

Nigel: Yeah, that might just work. It would definitely make our stand visible and I'm sure word would get around.

Thomas: Hmm, not a bad idea and sorry to be negative, but I don't think it'll work. I've been manning the stand now for some ten years. While refreshments is a good idea, if someone's going to or from a meeting they're usually in a hurry and even if they do stop to grab a water or something, they're not going to be interested in one of us giving them a sales pitch. Plus, how are we going to make sure that we don't run out of refreshments on day one? I think logistically, it could be a real problem.

Nigel: Maybe we should spend a bit more time on this outside the conference call. Can I leave this with you, Martin? I'm sure we can come up with something suitable!

Martin: Sure, no problem. I'll give it some thought and email you my suggestions, if that sounds OK.

Nigel: Sure thing. Thanks, a lot, Martin. Bye!

Thomas: Bye, Martin. Look forward to hearing from you later.

Martin: Bye Nigel, bye Thomas. I'll be in touch!

12. Happy Sweets Plc

Rosa: Hello. Swindon Delivers. Rosa speaking.

Melanie: Hello, I'm calling from Happy Sweets Plc in Bourton.

Rosa: Ah, hello. How can I help you?

Melanie: Would you be able to give me a quote for an urgent parcel to Portugal?

Rosa: Certainly. Do you have the destination city or town, plus the approximate parcel dimensions and weight?

Melanie: Yes, the city's Lisbon. The parcel dimensions are thirty centimetres by twenty centimetres by fifteen centimetres and it weighs about twenty kilos.
Rosa: OK. And would we be picking up the parcel from your Bourton offices?
Melanie: Yes, please.
Rosa: Our quickest door-to-door service to Lisbon by European Road Freight would take two to three working days and would cost seventy-five pounds plus VAT.
Melanie: Would the parcel definitely take two days? It's very urgent, so the sooner it can get there, the better.
Rosa: I'm sorry, but I can't guarantee that the parcel will definitely take two days. There could be delays at customs, etc, which might slow things down. The problem is, you never know.
Melanie: I see. So, does the price include insurance?
Rosa: Yes, it covers a standard liability of up to fifty pounds. You can opt for additional insurance liability to cover you against loss or damage of your shipment, if you like. For a hundred pounds more, we will pay you fifty euros per kilogram for all shipments over ten kilos.
Melanie: What exactly does that mean?
Rosa: Well, it means that if your parcel gets lost or is damaged, we'll pay you compensation of fifty euros for each kilogram your parcel weighs, which in your case would be a thousand euros.
Melanie: Oh, I see. And what other services do you offer?
Rosa: You're given a tracking number so that you can track your consignment online. Once the consignment's been delivered, we'll also email you a copy of the proof of delivery for your records.
Melanie: Thanks very much for your help. I'll get back to you later on today if we decide to go ahead with the shipment.
Rosa: Thank you, goodbye.
Melanie: Bye!

KT Couriers: Hello, KT Couriers?
Melanie: Yes, hello. I need a quote for an urgent parcel.
KT Couriers: Have you visited our website? There you can get an online quote.
Melanie: Sorry, but I haven't got the time to fill in forms.
KT Couriers: OK, so where are you calling from?
Melanie: From Happy Sweets Plc in Bourton.
KT Couriers: Do you have the consignment details there, such as destination, weight and size of the parcel, etc?
Melanie: Yes, the parcel's to be sent to Lisbon in Portugal. It weighs twenty kilos and is thirty centimetres by twenty centimetres by fifteen centimetres.
KT Couriers: And which service would you require? Our quickest service would be airfreight.
Melanie: Am I right in assuming that that would include collection from our office and delivery to the client's door?
KT Couriers: Yes, that's right.
Melanie: How long would airfreight take?
KT Couriers: With airfreight, your parcel will be delivered next day.
Melanie: Well, the parcel's extremely urgent, so I think we'd have to opt for airfreight. How much would it cost?
KT Couriers: That would be two hundred and fifty pounds plus VAT.
Melanie: And what about insurance?
KT Couriers: Included in the quote is our standard liability which covers the full value of the consignment plus the shipping costs if the consignment is lost or damaged. Additional insurance can be purchased, if required.
Melanie: What other benefits are there if I were to use your company?
KT Couriers: Well, you can track your consignment online using our tracking system which allows you to follow the delivery status of your parcel in real-time. As soon as something happens to your parcel, you see it immediately on screen. All relevant documents, such as delivery notes and proofs of delivery can be viewed online and downloaded. You can also book the collection online and print out the necessary bar code labels, so that we just need to pick up. Plus we have an email notification service. As soon as your parcel's been signed for, an email advising you of successful delivery will be automatically sent to you.
Melanie: Is it OK, if I call you back later? I've spoken to other forwarding companies so I just need to compare quotes.
KT Couriers: Of course, not a problem. Thanks for calling.
Melanie: Goodbye!
KT Couriers: Goodbye.

13. Dealing with a complaint

Ian: Good afternoon, thank you for calling Healthy Sleep. How can I help you?
Fredericke: Good afternoon. This is Fredericke Wunderlich calling from Süße Träume in Germany.
Ian: Ah, hello, Ms Wunderlich! How are you today?
Fredericke: Well, to be honest, I'm not very happy.
Ian: I'm sorry to hear that. What seems to be the problem?
Fredericke: Well, we placed a large order with you last month. We received the consignment from you today, five days late, by the way and when we checked it we found that some of it was either wrong, faulty or missing. It's just not good enough!
Ian: Oh dear. Let me look into this. Do you have the order number, please?
Fredericke: Yes, it's ST zero two three five six, dated the sixth of March.
Ian: OK, that was an order for twenty-five of our "Sleep Well" double beds and ten single beds from our Dreamtime range.
Fredericke: Yes, that's right. But we only got five beds from the "Sleep Well" range and those were the wrong size: king

size instead of double. The remaining twenty double beds were from another collection, Nomad, it says on the delivery note. We didn't even order those!

Ian: And what about the rest of the order?

Fredericke: The single beds from the Dreamtime range arrived, but five of them were damaged and the other five were incomplete. We have the frames but no bed bases.

Ian: What exactly was the damage on the single beds? I'll need this information so that I can fill in a complaint form and pass it on to our production department for actioning.

Fredericke: They're marked and chipped and generally of poor quality.

Ian: Do you think that the beds could have been damaged during transit?

Fredericke: No, I don't think so as the consignment arrived with no visible signs of damage and all units were sealed and shrink-wrapped.

Ian: I'm really sorry about this. We'll investigate what could have gone wrong. As you know, we try our best to maintain the highest levels of quality at all times, so I'm surprised that this happened.

Fredericke: Yes, me too. As a long-standing client of yours, this is the first time that I've been unhappy with a delivery. Hopefully, it'll be the last time too!

Ian: As regards the rest of your order, we've recently installed a new software program at our warehouse and we've been having a few problems with it. You're not the first customer to contact us with such a complaint though we've since implemented a series of checks to ensure no further warehousing errors occur.

Fredericke: Well, that would explain the incorrect and missing items, I suppose. But what I need to know is what will be done about this. I have customers who have been waiting for their order to come from you, and now they have to wait even longer.

Ian: OK, what I'll do is generate a purchase order for the faulty items right away. I see here that they're part of our standard stock, so you won't have to wait more than two working days for them. In the meantime, we'll arrange for our freight forwarder to collect the incorrect items from your warehouse and deliver the replacement items.

Fredericke: OK, but what about my customers who still have to wait for their orders?

Ian: I can arrange for a discount on your account for this order so you can pass this on to your customers as a goodwill gesture.

Fredericke: They won't be happy, but I guess that's the only thing that we can do. How much do you suggest?

Ian: How about a ten percent reduction? I'm extremely sorry for the mix-up, but now your order should be with you in a couple of days.

Fredericke: OK. Thank you for your help and I hope I don't have to call back!

Ian: Thank you for calling. Goodbye Frau Wunderlich.

Fredericke: Goodbye.

14. Taking minutes

Dieter: Hello, I'm Dieter Schmitt and I'd like to thank Anna Hanson and George McFowler from our New York office and Chris Nettles from our Nottingham office for attending this year's management review. To my right is Simon Wölfe, he's my personal assistant and he'll be taking notes during the meeting.
As you all know, this past year has been a difficult one for us, not least due to increasing energy costs across the company. Profits are down and as a result, I've called you all together today to discuss what common measures we are going to implement to keep costs down. So, who would like to set the ball rolling? How about you, George?

George: Well, I was thinking that we should carry out a review of all our suppliers and see if we can negotiate better deals with them or alternatively, find new suppliers. This will obviously have to be done on a country by country basis, but might just help to reduce costs across the company. It's also the obvious place to start.

Anna: I think that's a great idea. We've been with some of our suppliers so long, they seem to think they can charge us what they like!

Dieter: Well, our buyers have just recently negotiated new terms with all our suppliers, so I don't think we can go back to them a second time.

Chris: We have contracts with all of our suppliers, so I'm not sure that we'll be in a position to negotiate, but I guess we can give it a try.

Anna: I also think we should reduce costs by closing some of our oldest and least efficient factories. It'll inevitably mean job losses, but sometimes drastic measures are needed.

Dieter: I think we should see factory closures as the last resort. If we need to shed jobs, then maybe a better way would be to ask for voluntary redundancies within the company? We'll be checking staffing levels here in Germany and if we find that they're too high, that's what we'll do.

Anna: Well, some of our plants are so old that in order to make them efficient they would require an enormous amount of investment. It would actually be much cheaper for us to close the worst performing factories. So I think factory closures are the answer. We could always ask staff to relocate to other sites instead.

Chris: All of our plants have the latest technology and can't be made any more efficient. Therefore, in the UK at least, I don't think closing factories would be a solution. At least, not just yet. A recruitment freeze would be worth trying in the short-term though until market conditions have stabilised a bit.

Anna: OK, a recruitment freeze could work for us and we can always review the decision again in six months time or so.

Dieter: Well I think we should adapt our factories so that they can run on fuel from renewable resources rather than fossil fuels. This will reduce our reliance on coal and make us less at risk to further price rises. Therefore, this is definitely something we'll be investing in Germany.

Chris: Using renewable resources takes investment and I'm not sure if it's something we should be doing at the moment.

George: Plus I'm not sure of the long-term gain. We all know that our plants require an enormous amount of energy that couldn't be satisfied by existing alternative energy sources.
Chris: I know it's not a top priority, but what about saving on travel expenses? In future, we could conduct a lot more of our meetings via video-conferencing rather than us having to travel from all over the world a couple of times a year. Plus it's not very environmentally friendly. Think of all that CO two! I don't think there are many things that we can say here today that we can't say in a video-conference. In future, I'll certainly be thinking twice before I travel anywhere on business.
Anna: While I agree with you on that one, Chris, I still think that it's important for us to all meet up face-to-face at least once a year. It's just not the same if you're down the end of a video link-up.
Dieter: I agree with you, Chris and I'll suggest that we put a cap on business travel here in the German office.
George: I don't know how you all feel about this, but maybe we should reduce our spend on marketing? Our corporate website's now up and running and our advertising campaign has been very successful, so I think maybe we should take this off our list of priorities and reinvest the money instead.
Dieter: Chris, you're from the UK headquarters. What do you think? All I know is that in Germany we have a steady market and a solid reputation.
Chris: Er, yes. I'll have to double-check, but in principle I think it would be good to spend less on marketing over the next year. Our marketing budget last year was huge, so I think some savings would have to be made here anyway.
Dieter: OK, we've got some good ideas there. I suggest we stop for a short break and then reconvene in, say, fifteen minutes?

15. Job interview

Tom Raitkin: Hello, Mr Smith. Thank you for coming in to see us today. My name's Tom Raitkin and I'm the Head of Sales. And this is my colleague, Betty Marsh, who's in charge of the HR department. She'll be here to take notes and ensure that the interview is held in accordance with company guidelines.
Martin Smith: Nice to meet you, Mr Raitkin. Hello, Mrs Marsh.
Tom Raitkin: So, to start off, please tell us a bit about yourself.
Martin Smith: Well, I'm Martin Smith. I'm currently Regional Sales Manager for Swanton & Co. in Newcastle.
Tom Raitkin: It says on your CV that you've been with Swanton for the past ten years. Why do you want to leave? You have a very good position there.
Martin Smith: Well, my wife has been offered and has accepted a job in Exeter, so rather than commute, we've decided to move away from Newcastle. Also, I've worked my way up through the company and feel as if I've achieved all I can with Swanton. I started there as a trainee and whilst I've really enjoyed my time there, I feel that it's time to move on. I'm managing a small team of six sales representatives, but there are no real opportunities to develop my career further, so I'm looking for a new challenge.
Tom Raitkin: So why do you want to join Sintra?
Martin Smith: Well, Sintra is a highly respected company within the industry and it's a large international company with offices around the world. I've heard that Sintra values good people and encourages them to develop their skills and I'm hoping that I'll be able to build upon my sales experience by working with clients and colleagues throughout Europe.
Tom Raitkin: Talking of which, do you speak any foreign languages?
Martin Smith: Yes, I studied French and Spanish at university. My Spanish is still OK, but my French is a bit rusty as I don't have much opportunity to use it in my current job.
Tom Raitkin: I gather from what you've said that it won't be a problem to relocate to Exeter. But what about the day-to-day demands of the job? We need someone who's very flexible for this position as there's a lot of travelling involved, some of which at the last minute. Would this be a problem?
Martin Smith: No, I realise that it's a necessary part of the job and to be honest, it's something that I'm looking forward to after being office-based for so long.
Tom Raitkin: As mentioned in our job advertisement the salary is negotiable depending upon experience. I see here that your salary at Swanton is thirty-eight thousand pounds.
Martin Smith: Yes, that's right. Ideally, I'd like to be earning a minimum of forty-two thousand pounds, plus would a company car be included in the package?
Tom Raitkin: In principle yes, but we'd need to confirm this once we've chosen the successful candidate, as I'm sure you understand.
Martin Smith: Yes, of course.
Tom Raitkin: So, Mr Smith, why do you think that you'd be suitable to work for Sintra?
Martin Smith: Well, I'm hard-working, a good team-player, highly organised and respected by my colleagues and bosses alike.
Tom Raitkin: So, if we were to offer you the job, when would you be able to start?
Martin Smith: I've got a three month notice period, so my first day with you would be the first of September.
Tom Raitkin: OK, so that's the end of the official part for now. Do you have any questions?
Martin Smith: No, I don't think so.
Tom Raitkin: OK, well, thank you very much for your time, Mr Smith. You'll be hearing from us shortly.
Martin Smith: Thank you very much. It's been nice meeting you both. Goodbye!
Tom Raitkin: Goodbye, Mr Smith.

mock exams

Niveaustufe 1

Thomas: Hi Kirsten, how are you today?
Kirsten: I'm fine, thanks Thomas. How are you?
Thomas: Not bad, though I need your help with something ...
Kirsten: OK, so how can I help?
Thomas: Well, you know that I'm going on a business trip tomorrow?
Kirsten: Do you mean to Holland?
Thomas: Yes, well, could you do me a favour and leave an out-of-office message in German on my voicemail?
Kirsten: Yes, of course. What would you like me to say?
Thomas: Well, can you say that I'm away on business from the twentieth to the twenty-third of April, and that I'll be back in the office on Monday, the twenty-sixth of April?
Kirsten: OK and do you want your calls to be forwarded to anyone in your absence?
Thomas: No, that's fine. Although do you think that you could check through any messages once or twice a day?
Kirsten: Yes, I can do that. So what if there's something urgent, is there another contact number you can be reached on?
Thomas: Yes, there's my mobile number: zero one seven six three two four five eight seven four one.
Kirsten: Right, got that. Do you want me to pass this number on to anyone who calls for you?
Thomas: Well, I'm waiting for some important calls from a few of my key customers, so you can pass on my mobile number to them.
Kirsten: OK, so who are you waiting to hear from, so that I can check if any messages come in for you?
Thomas: Well, there's Tony Smith from KT Limited, Sam Finch from YTS and Dave Hammond from Target.
Kirsten: OK, so if any of them call, I'll give them your mobile phone number, right?
Thomas: Yes, that's right.
Kirsten: OK, I'll get onto it right away, Thomas. Have a nice business trip!
Thomas: Thanks, Kirsten.

Niveaustufe 2

Toni: Lampenfieber GmbH. Guten Tag, Herr Schmidt am Apparat.
David: Hello, Mr Schmidt. This is David Duggins from Duggins Ltd, Bournemouth.
Toni: Ah, hello, Mr Duggins. What can I do for you?
David: Well unfortunately I'm ringing to complain about our last order.
Toni: Oh, I'm sorry to hear that. Do you have your customer reference number, Mr Duggins?
David: Yes, it's GB zero two five three.
Toni: I'll just get your customer details up on our database. OK, so that's David Duggins, Duggins Ltd, four three two Main Street, Bournemouth, BH one two LW.
David: Yes, that's right.
Toni: Do you have the order number, please?
David: It's DG four eight two nine.
Toni: Thank you. OK, so that's your order dated twenty-fifth of May, delivered to your warehouse today. So, what appears to be the problem with the order, Mr Duggins?
David: Well, the warehouse is still checking the order which came in this morning, but so far they think that about a half of the order is damaged.
Toni: Oh dear. I'm really sorry about that. Do you have any more details?
David: Well, we don't think that it was a manufacturing fault, as it's only crates which are damaged on the outside which seem to be affected.
Toni: The crates were damaged on the outside? But they were checked here before they left our warehouse and they were fine.
David: Yes, my contact here said that the freight forwarder dropped some of the crates during unloading, so we think that must be the reason though we won't know for sure until we've gone through the whole consignment.
Toni: OK, then. Once you've done that, please could you send me a fax with all the details of the damaged stock, number of crates, product numbers, etc?
David: Yes, certainly. I'll get my people in the warehouse onto it straightaway.
Toni: Once we've got your fax, we'll send out the replacement stock to you and collect the damaged goods so that we can take a look at them here.
David: And how long would it take for the replacement stock to get to us? About two days?
Toni: Yes, that's right. Our usual delivery time is two days.
David: Would it be possible to send the stock to us by courier for next day delivery? We have quite a lot of customers here waiting for these items.
Toni: Yes, we can do that, but I'll need to get your fax with the details of all damaged stock within the next couple of hours so that I can make the necessary arrangements.
David: OK, thanks for your help, Mr Schmidt. I'll send you a fax in the next couple of hours.
Toni: Thanks, Mr Duggins. Bye for now.
David: Bye Toni.

Niveaustufe 3

Fredrik: Hello, I'm Fredrik Broberg and this is my colleague, Elisabet Hanssen. We're from Toys Direct B.V. and we have an appointment at ten am with Mr Lohmann.

Sabine: Hello Mr Broberg, hello Mrs Hanssen. Welcome to Spielzeugwelt. Here are your security passes. I'll take you to Mr Lohmann. If you'd both like to follow me.

Sabine: Did you have a good journey here?

Elisabet: Yes, thank you. We took the overnight ferry from Gothenburg and then the train from Kiel, so it was a bit long, about fifteen hours, but we're here now!

Sabine: So, are you staying in Germany for a couple of days, or will you be returning to Sweden after the meeting?

Fredrik: We'll be in Germany for a few days as we have appointments with some other companies here.

Elisabet: We've got a hotel booked here in Hamburg tonight and then tomorrow we'll be in Berlin for two days. I'm really looking forward to being in Berlin!

Sabine: Oh yes, Berlin's a great city. I'm sure you'll enjoy your time there.

Fredrik: Do you have any idea how long the meeting's scheduled to last? I have to make an urgent call at lunchtime so I might need to be excused for a while.

Sabine: Well, we've reserved the meeting room for you from ten till two, but there will be a break for lunch at about twelve. We are going to take you to a really good German restaurant for lunch, but I think you'll have time within the hour break to make your call. Does that sound alright?

Fredrik: Yes, that sounds great.

Sabine: Your company's based just outside Gothenburg isn't it?

Elisabet: Yes, that's right. It's in a place called Mölndal, about five kilometres south of Gothenburg.

Sabine: Well, we're here now. Mr Broberg, Mrs Hanssen, this is Mr Lohmann, our Managing Director. Mr Lohmann, this is Mr Broberg and this is Mrs Hanssen from Toys Direct.

Mr Lohmann: Nice to see you both. Right, I suggest that we get straight down to business. So could you tell me a bit more about your company? I've heard of you of course, but if we want to work together I'd need to know a lot more.

Elisabet: Well, our company, Toys Direct is actually an old Swedish company, despite its modern sounding name. The company is over one hundred and fifty years old and has been owned by generations of the Amdahlsson family. Originally it had a Swedish name, but that was changed to Toys Direct some twenty years ago when the company opened up to the international and worldwide markets.

Mr Lohmann: And can you give me an idea of the size of your company?

Fredrik: Over the past ten years Toy Direct's grown massively due in part to a high volume of business over the internet. Currently we have two thousand five hundred staff spread over two sites. We have our Headquarters in Mölndal, just outside of Gothenburg. Mölndal is home to our sales, logistics, accounting, human resources and IT divisions and has approximately one thousand seven hundred and fifty staff. Then we have a manufacturing facility (including production, design and quality control teams) near Karlstad which employs some seven hundred and fifty people.

Mr Lohmann: I see. So, you're interested in a possible cooperation. Why did you choose us at Spielzeugwelt?

Fredrik: Yes, that's right. Well, we're the leading toy manufacturer in Sweden and throughout Scandinavia. Despite our internet sales, we haven't really got a presence on the German market, so we're interested in finding partners in Germany who would be prepared to introduce our products onto the German market, selling them under license from us. In return, we'd promote your products in Scandinavia. Our research showed that your company has the biggest toy sales in Germany, so we thought that you'd be well placed to help us.

Elisabet: Also, your company has an excellent reputation in the industry for quality. We do too. All our toys are made from trees from managed forests in Sweden and are of the highest quality. In order to compete with cheap, plastic imports, we need to work together with other like-minded companies.

Fredrik: Yes, that's right.

Mr Lohmann: OK. Well, I suggest we take a short coffee break and continue in ten minutes. How does that sound?

REZEPTION

1. Taking a message

Anruf angenommen von: Susanne Müller; **Anruf für:** Anne Wilke **Anrufer (Name und Firma):** Tony Miller, Office to go; **Telefonnummer:** 0044 20 856 951; **Referenznummer:** BD 456 QW 12; **Grund des Anrufs:** Herr Miller möchte zusätzliche Artikel (zu der gestrigen Bestellung) bestellen

2. Rooms available

1. 23. - 26. Juli; **2.** sechs Zimmer: Zwei Doppelzimmer und vier Einzelzimmer; **3.** Ein Doppelzimmer und zwei Einzelzimmer; **4.** £135 pro Nacht; **5.** Edinburgh Park Hotel; **6.** 01254 578963

3. Office supplies

Customer: DFG Logistics; **Paper:** 10 boxes of inkjet; size: A4 **Labels:** 14 packets; colour: light blue; **Envelopes:** Colour: white; size: A4; amount: 3000 (6 packets); Colour: brown; size: A5; amount: 1000;
Pens: Colours: blue and black; 3 boxes at 80 per box;
Delivery time: tomorrow morning, 9 o'clock

4. Preparing for a meeting

1. Mary-Ellen; **2.** USB-Sticks; Computer-Mäuse; **3.** In einem griechischen Restaurant; **4.** Er ernährt sich gesund.; **5.** Nüsse

5. Problems with a delivery

1. Ted Hoskins, 34 Station Road, Guildford, GU1 3WR, Great Britain; **2.** QWE1452; **3.** 0044 115 473 214; **4.** Er hat vor 3 Wochen über das Internet bestellt; **5.** Er hat einen Schrank namens Lava in Birke und eine Kommode namens Volt, dunkelblau bestellt; **6.** seinen Anwalt einzuschalten.

6. Telephone query

1. Buchhaltung; **2.** Frau Thomas; **3.** eine überfällige Rechnung; **4.** sofortige Überweisung/Morehouse soll Rechnung noch einmal faxen; **5.** Firma bezahlt normalerweise pünktlich.

7. Stock control

Name: Mike Dalton; **Niederlassung:** UK; **Geräte:**
Modell: Vision65; **Anzahl:** 250; **Preis:** £1499
Modell: 32LD; **Anzahl:** 100; **Preis:** £1800
Modell: DanceMaster 5000; **Anzahl:** 300 orange, 300 schwarz; **Preis:** £295
Modell: HiFi2034 Powerstation; **Anzahl:** 1000; **Preis:** £99
Modell: iWalk station W752; **Anzahl:** 500; **Preis:** £450
Lieferung: bis zum 15. Oktober im Lager; **Sonstiges:** bitte an das Lager in Reading, nicht in Basingstoke schicken, z. Hd. Les Hooper

8. Email for you

(in Stichwörtern)
1. David Green; **2.** Because it takes time to deal with a large number of emails and people might forget about their other work priorities.; **3.** Only read and answer emails twice a day./Use labelling options/ Review the sender and the subject matter/Delete emails that aren't relevant to job/Delete junk email/Unsubscribe from mass mailings/Ask to be taken off unnecessary distribution lists.; **4.** You need to abide by your company's email protocol./Need to make sure that you don't write anything personal, sexist, racist or rude in an email as it could mean that you lose your job./Is not informal, is still business correspondence./Possible danger to overuse email.

9. Travel itinerary

Purpose of visit: business trip (to visit some fitness studios in the US); **Day 1, Flight from:** London Heathrow **to:** New York, JFK, **Departure:** 15.40, **Arrival:** 18.15, **Hotel:** Queen's hotel, **Appointments:** None; **Day 2, City:** New York, **Appointments:** Mark Davids, MidTown Gym, 4pm, Jean Middler, Central Gym, 4.30pm; Betty Jones, New York Fitness Co., 5.30pm; **Day 3, Flight from:** New York, LaGuardia **to:** Chicago, **Departure:** 7am, **Arrival:** 9.35am, **Hotel:** Grand Mid-Western, **Appointments:** Phil Marks, Power Ladies Gym, 11.00; **Day 4, Flight from:** Chicago **to:** Denver, **Departure:** 8.25am, **Arrival:** 9.55, **Hotel:** Park Hotel, **Appointments:** Denise, Get Fit, 6pm; **Day 5, Flight from:** Denver **to:** London Heathrow, **Departure:** 16.50, **Arrival:** 11.15

10. Finding a conference room

1. Wo ist der Raum? Zentral-London, 5 Minuten zu Fuß Paddington Station; **Preis:** £480 pro Tag; **Personenzahl:** 16; **Verpflegung:** Tee, Kaffee und Kekse bei Ankunft, in den Vormittags- und Nachmittagspausen, Sandwichs und alkoholfreie Getränke zu Mittag; **Welche Extras sind im Preis enthalten?** 42-Zoll Plasma Bildschirm, DVD-Spieler; **Sonstiges:** Wein kostet extra
2. Wo ist der Raum? Westlondon, 500 yards von der Shepherds Bush U-Bahn Station; **Preis:** £650; **Personenzahl:** 20; **Verpflegung:** Empfangsgetränke, Tee, Kaffee, Wasser und Kekse und ein warmes Büfett; **Welche Extras sind im Preis enthalten?** W-LAN Internet, Video-Konferenz; **Sonstiges:** 10% Rabatt bei einer Reservierung zwei Monate im Voraus

11. Preparations for the trade fair

1. Vom 1. - 8. April; **2.** 2000; **3.** Der Aufbau findet zwei Tage vor Messebeginn an; Sechs Mitarbeiter; **4.** Erfrischungen am Stand; **5.** Seit 10 Jahren; **6.** Die Leute sind in Eile/Wer sorgt dafür, dass es immer Erfrischungen gibt? (ein logistisches Problem)

12. Happy Sweets Plc

(in Stichwörtern)
Swindon Delivers
Überland; 2 bis 3 Werktage; £75 plus MwSt.; können nicht garantieren, dass das Paket in 2 Tagen da ist; Haftungsnorm bis £50; zusätzliche Versicherung gegen Verlust und Beschädigung kann abgeschlossen werden; für £100 extra erhält man 50 € pro kg für alle Pakete über 10 kg; man erhält eine Identifikationsnummer; kann damit online den Weg des Pakets nachvollziehen; nach Lieferung erhält man eine Bestätigung per E-Mail
KT Couriers
Luftpost - Lieferung am nächsten Tag; £250 plus MwSt; Haftungsnorm: voller Wert der Sendung plus Versandkosten, falls Sendung verloren geht oder beschädigt wird; Sendung kann online nachverfolgt werden; alle notwendigen Dokumente können heruntergeladen werden; Abholung kann online gebucht werden und Barcodes können ausgedruckt werden; sobald für die Lieferung unterschrieben wurde erhält man eine Bestätigung per E-Mail
Besseres Angebot: KT Couriers (weil die Lieferung dringend ist)

13. Dealing with a complaint

(in Stichwörtern)
25 Doppelbetten Sleep Well und 10 Einzelbetten aus der Dreamtime Reihe wurden bestellt; nur 5 Betten Sleep Well wurden geliefert; diese waren falsche Größe (zu groß); die anderen 20 Betten waren aus einer anderen Reihe (Nomad); die Einzelbetten aus der Dreamtime Reihe wurden zwar geliefert, aber fünf davon waren beschädigt und bei 5 fehlten Teile

14. Taking minutes

(in Stichwörtern)

1. alle Zulieferer überprüfen; versuchen bessere Konditionen zu vereinbaren oder neue Zulieferer zu finden
2. Fabriken auf den neuesten Stand zu bringen wäre zu teuer; Schließen wäre billiger
3. weniger Geschäftsreisen zu machen; Reisekosten zu sparen
4. Umweltschutz
5. Firmenwebsite läuft; Werbekampagne war erfolgreich

15. Job interview

Full name of interviewee: Martin Smith; **Present employment:** Regional Sales Manager; **Current employer:** Swanton & Co.; **Reasons for wanting to leave current position:** Wife has job in Exeter so family is relocating; No real opportunities to progress; **Reasons for wanting to join Sintra Ltd:** Highly respected company; Large international company with offices around the world; Values good people and encourages development; Wants to build upon his sales experience; **Language skills:** Spanish - good. French a bit rusty; **Mobility/flexibility:** Will relocate/happy to be flexible; **Salary expectations:** £42,000; **Earliest date for commencement of job:** 1st September (3 months' notice period)

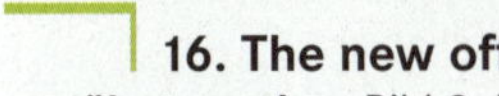

16. The new office

erwähnt werden: Bild 2, Bild 5, Bild 6, Bild 7, Bild 8, Bild 10, Bild 11, Bild 13, Bild 15

17. An order by telephone

a 7; b 3; c 1; d 8; e 10; f 2; g 4; h 12; i 9; j 6; k 11; l 5

18. Job descriptions

1. d; 2. c; 3. g; 4. b; 5. i; 6. e; 7. h; 8. a; 9. f

19. Facts & Figures

Myers & Miller Factsheet
Produkte: verschiedene Säfte und nicht-alkoholische Softdrinks; **Hauptsitz:** Brisbane, Australien; **Filialen:** in ganz Australien den USA und Kanada; **Mitarbeiter:** 11 000; **Kunden:** Großhändler, Supermärkte, Hotels, Fluggesellschaften, Restaurantketten, Kreuzfahrtschiffe; **Werbung (Werbestrategien):** Sportveranstaltungen sponsern; Fernsehwerbung; Werbeaktionen mit kostenlosen Proben;
Umsatz: 235 Millionen Euro; **Art des Unternehmens:** privates Familienunternhemen; **Geschäftsführer:** Brendan Myers

20. Ordering online

a)5; b)1; c)7; d)8; e)2; f)4; g)6; h)3

21. How (not) to behave

1. yes; **2.** could choose between 30 different descriptions of bad behaviour; **3.** a) no; b) no; c) yes; d) yes; e) yes; f) yes; g) yes; **4.** 615 employees and university staff and students from Baltimore

22. Business travel

a) false; b) true; c) false; d) true; e) true;
1. No, it isn't. **2.** They do not want the ban of phone calls in-flight lifted. **3.** They affect concentration and attention; stress you; impact on health generally

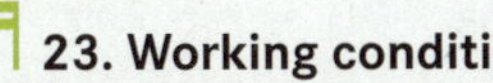

23. Working conditions

1. No, although that used to be the case. Now the salary should cover all expenses though there might be bonuses.; **2.** No, you can use it to save money and live the high life.; **3.** No, some companies regularly delay the payment of salaries.; **4.** No, you'll receive eight months' salary (one month's salary per year of employment).; **5.** Yes, they are. Thursday is less common.; **6.** Yes, they do. The school "weekend" is Thursday and Friday.
Correct answers:
1. Since there are no personal taxes in Dubai, people have a higher income in general.; **2.** According to the law, indemnity payments have to be paid to employees who fulfilled their contracts.;
3. Muslims only have to work six hours per day during Ramadan.

24. Ordering office supplies

1976; Price Club; converted airplane hangar in San Diego;
1983; first Costco warehouse; Seattle; $0 – 3 billion in 6 years
1993; merger of Costco and Price Club, new name PriceCostco; 206 locations; $16 billion
1997; Costco; worldwide; $50 billion
Types of membership
Executive – benefits: 2 % annual reward on most Costco purchases, additional benefits on member services such as lower prices on auto financing; **target group/category:** highest level of membership; **membership fee:** not mentioned
Business – benefits: one household card, additional Business Membership cards are available for $40 each; **target group/category:** all licensed businesses, non-profit organizations, government agencies; **membership fee:** $50 per year, Additional Business Membership cards are available for $40 each
Gold Star – benefits: one household card; **target group/category:** available for individuals who do not qualify for a Business Membership; **membership fee:** $50 per year

25. A job in the USA

OFFICO
Branche: Großhändler von Büromaterialien; **Dauer des Vertrages:** befristet; **Arbeitsumfang (Voll/Teil):** Teilzeit; **Arbeitsort:** Chicago; **Kontaktmöglichkeit für Bewerbung:** Anruf an Bernard Smythe für telefonisches Vorstellungsgespräch, Telefonnummer: 386-3440; **Stundenlohn:** $ 10 – 14; **Tätigkeiten:** Kundenanfragen per Telefon und E-Mail beantworten, Buchhaltung, Bestellungen schreiben
besondere Fähigkeiten/Erfahrung/Abschlüsse, die man mitbringen sollte: Organisationstalent und Kenntnisse über Buchhaltung, Arbeitserfahrung (1 Jahr) in Büroumfeld; sicherer Umgang mit Microsoft Office
Leistungen für die Mitarbeiter:
Besonderheiten der Stelle: Wochenendarbeit; Auto benötigt

Summers & Sons
Branche: Autohändler; **Dauer des Vertrages:** unbefristet; **Arbeitsumfang (Voll/Teil):** Teilzeit; **Arbeitsort:** Modesto; **Kontaktmöglichkeit für Bewerbung:** Bewerbung an Personalchef Mr Kilter; **Stundenlohn:** $11; **Tätigkeiten:** Telefon beantworten; Termine machen; Ablage; Faxe versenden; Kopieren; **besondere Fähigkeiten/Erfahrung/Abschlüsse, die man mitbringen sollte:** Spanisch fließend; sicherer Umgang mit Excel; High School Abschluss; **Leistungen für die Mitarbeiter:** Weiterbildung; **Besonderheiten der Stelle:** flexible Arbeitszeiten, Überstunden

MIRANA
Branche: Software Unternehmen; **Dauer des Vertrages:** unbefristet; **Arbeitsumfang (Voll/Teil):** Voll; **Arbeitsort:** New York; **Kontaktmöglichkeit für Bewerbung:** E-Mail an Personalchef (val. james@sid-wvd.com); **Stundenlohn:** $11-15; **Tätigkeiten:** Treffen arrangieren, Reiseplanung, Messeorganisation, allg. Sekretariatsaufgaben; **besondere Fähigkeiten/Erfahrung/Abschlüsse, die man mitbringen sollte:** sehr gute Organisationsfähigkeiten und im Stande sein schnell zu arbeiten; **Leistungen für die Mitarbeiter:** Betriebsrente; **Besonderheiten der Stelle:** Geschäftsreisen können vorkommen

26. Career choice: secretary

Aufgabenbereiche: Informationsmanagement, Termine der Mitarbeiter arrangieren, Verwaltung, Datenbankmanagement, Kommunikation persönlich und am Telefon
Ausbildung: sollten Tastschreiben und Textverarbeitung von Beginn an beherrschen, evtl. College Ausbildung, Fremdsprachenkenntnisse von Vorteil
erforderliche Kenntnisse (z. B. Software): sicherer Umgang mit neuester Technologie
Chancen für berufliche Weiterentwicklung: Austausch mit anderen Sekretär/innen kann helfen, Arbeitserfahrung kann bei Berufswechsel helfen, mit Berufserfahrung auch Wechsel in spezialisierte Berufe (z. B. Redaktion, Buchhaltung) möglich
Vor- und Nachteile von Zeit/Leiharbeit: Zeitarbeit: flexibel and abwechslungsreich, aber auch Routine und Unverlässlichkeit

1. Ein Sekretär/eine Sekretärin muss sich mit aktuellen Software Programmen und Büroausrüstung (Kopierer, Computer etc.) auskennen.
2. Sekretär/innen sind oft die ersten Ansprechpartner für Außenstehenden.
3. Gute Sekretär/innen warten nicht darauf, dass sie Anweisungen erhalten - sie ergreifen die Initiative.
4. Ein allgemeiner Ausdruck, der viele Komponenten beinhaltet.

27. New ways in advertising

Merkblatt: Handywerbung
Größe des Markts: $871 Millionen weltweit, im Moment klein, aber könnte bis 2011 zwischen $11.4–$20 Milliarden erreichen
Art der Werbung: SMS, Werbung neben Videoclips, Websites, Downloads von Musik und Spielen
Potenzielle Wirkung: könnte Internet und sogar TV, Radio und gedruckte Werbung verdrängen
Vorteile: 2,5 Milliarden Handys; viel größeres Publikum als PCs; Anzahl an Handys nimmt stetig zu (schneller als PCs), vor allem in ärmeren Ländern; Handy hat man immer dabei; Werbung kann genauer fokusiert werden - Werbung entsprechend der Gewohnheiten des Kunden
Nachteile: Handys sind privat; Werbung könnte als Eindringen in Privatssphäre gewertet werden und Kunden abschrecken; in einigen Ländern nicht akzeptiert (z. B. Europa und Amerika) evtl. Datenschutzprobleme; nicht klar wie Gewinn erzielt bzw. verteilt werden soll zwischen Anbietern und Werbenden
Viele sind der Ansicht, dass wegen der momentanen Probleme, Handywerbung in nächster Zeit eine Randerscheinung bleiben wird.

28. A modern way to get a job

1. Zu Hause mit einer Kamera üben; überlegen wie man bequem und professionell sitzen kann; sich keine Gedanken über die Technik machen; drauf Konzentrieren was man erreichen möchte; so viel wie möglich über den Arbeitgeber herausfinden; die Website des Unternehmens zu Informationszwecken nutzen; Fachzeitschriften und Zeitungen lesen; sich über den Einstellungsvorgang informieren
2. professionell anziehen, wie für ein normales Interview; helle Farben vermeiden;
3. nicht unbedingt;
4. Ja; Notizblock und Stift mitnehmen
5. Nein; Hände und Körper ruhig halten;
6. viele Pausen machen; ruhig bleiben; nicht einfach irgendwas sagen
7. versuchen die Antwort so positiv wie möglich darzustellen
8. Ja, aber darum bitten später darauf zurück zu kommen wenn nötig

29. Tips for working abroad

1. true; 2. true; 3. false; 4. false; 5. false

1. Broaden cultural horizon, improve career prospects
2. Your profession and the ability to find suitable work there, quality of life achievable, the likely employment prospects, the affordability of that country in relation to the amount you can realistically earn
3. visas, permits, permissions, approvals
4. Some translate like-for-like, some have to be translated. It might also be possible that people have to apply to have their qualifications recognised or to take exams or tests

30. Business meetings

1. Stay concentrated, keep the topic of the meeting in mind, try to move forward and do not lose time with unimportant matters
2. colleagues who need to be there either because of their role or their knowledge of/involvement in the issue.
3. establish the ground rules for the meeting which are namely: to minimize confusion and disruptions and to institute a code of conduct
4. Sarcasm, personal attacks, interrupting, dominating the discussion, or engaging in distracting behaviour
5. to confront a person or group with ideas or a proposal when they don't expect it, to take them by surprise.

1. true; 2. true; 3. false; 4. true; 5. false; 6. true

PRODUKTION

1. Writing about work

(Musterlösung)
I am a full-time sales executive. I start work at 8.30 am every day. I read and write emails, letters and faxes every day and answer the phone. I deal with clients' queries, orders and complaints. I have lunch at midday. Sometimes in the afternoon I have to attend a meeting, but otherwise, I send quotes to clients and speak to them on the phone. I finish work at 6.30 pm, but on a Friday I finish at lunchtime.

2. Office party

(Musterlösung)
Dear Sir or Madam
I am writing regarding a booking made by my company on the 15th September. I am afraid that the party has been postponed by two months meaning that the original date of the 30th March has been moved to the 30th May. I am terribly sorry that the order has had to be postponed and I apologise for any trouble caused.
There are also some changes to the menu. We previously asked for 40 veal cutlets, 100 sausages and 80 chicken drumsticks. We would now like to order 60 veal cutlets, 85 sausages, 30 salmon steaks and 120 chicken drumsticks. The rest of the menu stays the same.
Please can you confirm the new prices as soon as possible. I would also appreciate it if you could send me confirmation of the order.
Once again I would like to apologise for the trouble caused.
Yours faithfully

3. Writing an order

(Musterlösung)
Dear Sir or Madam
I am writing from Movies, a removal company based in Bristol. We should like to place an order with you for the following items:

- 30 silver doorstops
- 20 black straps at 5m each
- 25 blue straps at 10m each
- 60 beige boxes (58 cm x 75 cm x 47 cm)
- 150 white boxes (30 cm x 40 cm x 50 cm)
- 50 grey boxes (45 cm x 30 cm x 65 cm)
- 25 grey locks
- 35 black combination locks.

We would be very grateful if you could deliver as soon as possible. Additionally, we would like to request a copy of the new catalogue for this year.
Yours faithfully

4. Discover Dresden

(Musterlösung)
Dear ...
We here at Imagination would like to invite you to Dresden as a thank you for a good working relationship.
The itinerary will be as follows:
Day 1: Arrival in Dresden; evening meal together at the Pulverturm
Day 2: A guided tour of the city
Day 3: A visit to the world-famous porcelain manufacturer, Meißner
Day 4: Departure
The proposed date for this trip is the 9th – 12th May. Naturally, we will provide accommodation for you free of charge in a comfortable hotel in Dresden city centre.
Please register to confirm your place by the 1st April.
Yours sincerely

5. Booking a hotel room

(Musterlösung)
Dear Sir or Madam
I am writing on behalf of P&T Textiles, Glasgow. I would like to book three single en suite rooms for the 18th–22nd October. Ideally, the rooms would include showers rather than baths. This booking is on a half-board basis, and two of the guests are vegetarian.
The guests will be arriving late in the evening. I could not find any information on the internet regarding your check-in times. Do you have a 24 hour check-in, or must we make special arrangements if arriving outside the regular hours?
I should also like to book the small conference room at the hotel. We will need it from 6pm to 8pm on the 21st October.
I would be grateful if you could let me know when you would like payment, and also if you could send me confirmation of this booking.
Yours faithfully

6. Writing an enquiry

(Musterlösung)
Office Universe
348 Riverwalk
Pewaukee
WI 53072
USA

(Date)

Dear Sir or Madam
I am writing from Office Exquisite in Frankfurt. Having found your address on the internet, we would like to propose a business partnership with you.
Allow me to give you more information about our company. Office Exquisite is the leading manufacturer of fine office furniture. Our main office is in Frankfurt, and we have a branch in Munich. We have been operating successfully across Europe for five years now. We plan to introduce our products into the American market, starting next year, and consequently we are looking for an uncompromising business partner to work with.
Enclosed is our catalogue so that you might gain an overview of our company.
I hope that you will consider this proposal, and I look forward to hearing from you soon.
Yours faithfully

7. Reply to an enquiry

(Musterlösung)
Dear Sir or Madam
Thank you very much for your enquiry regarding the possibilities of a business partnership. We are very interested in both the products you offer and a potential business relationship.
We would like to know whether there is a bulk discount for bulk orders. We would also like information about your delivery times and existing delivery terms. Lastly, we would be very grateful if you could inform us about your payment terms.
We thank you again for your enquiry, and hope that we will be able to reach a mutually beneficial arrangement.
Yours faithfully

8. The new TX7

(Musterlösung)
Dear Ladies and Gentleman
Finding your dream car has never been so easy! Hachenberg Dealership is proud to announce that it is one of the very few car dealerships which have been allowed to invite chosen guests to an exclusive preview of the new TX7 model.
As you are longstanding customers of ours, we would like to extend this invitation to you. The preview is planned for the 14th April 20...
The event itself will start at 11 am with a champagne reception and snacks. This will be followed by a short speech from the managing director and the unveiling of the TX7. Between 12 and 5 pm, you'll have the one-off chance to take the TX7 on a 30-minute test-drive. An exclusive dinner, starting at 6pm, will round off this exciting day.
Places are limited, so please respond as soon as possible if you wish to secure yourself a place at the preview.
I look forward to seeing you at the event.
Yours sincerely

9. Writing an acknowledgement of order

(Musterlösung)
Dear Mr Hamilton
Thank you for your order of bathroom items received yesterday. The following items will be despatched to you at the beginning of next week:

- 30 bath mats, "Big Foot", blue, article no. 829/4935, unit price, 4.99 €
- 15 toilet seats, aqua frosted, article no. 832/0218, unit price, 15.95 €
- 50 brush holders, stainless steel, article no. 830/1970, unit price, 12.50 €
- 80 towel rails, chrome plated, article no. 831/0039, unit price, 6.30 €

Unfortunately, we are unable to fulfil part of the order: the shower curtain, "Friendly fish", article no. 830/1385, unit price 16.75 €, is currently out of stock. The manufacturer has informed us that the delivery time of this particular curtain might take up to five weeks. We will, of course, let you know as soon as the desired item becomes available. If for some reason you cannot wait this long, we recommend that you consider another model, for example, "Dolphin" (article number 830/1389). We will offer this with a 15% discount, although we should inform you that we only have limited stock of this item, too and can only fulfil this part of the order depending on incoming orders, and only for as long as stocks last. We apologise for any inconvenience caused and hope to hear from you soon.
Yours sincerely

10. Describing departments of a company

(Musterlösung)

Personnel deals with the selection of individuals for a job, and looks after their training and development. It is also responsible for keeping a record of employees' personal data and deals with pensions, bonuses and the like.

Purchasing negotiates prices, terms and conditions with suppliers. They select which suppliers to work with and give contracts to. They then take care of budgeting material costs, and are responsible, having formed a particular strategy, for closing the deal with the suppliers.

Sales is more concerned with customer relations. They send quotes to customers, deal with complaints and orders and attempt to secure new customers for the company.

Dispatch is responsible for getting orders to customers. The people there have to deal with the logistics of arranging the transport of goods to customers, so they organise the freight handling and all necessary paperwork, etc.

Accounts works with the financial side of the business. It checks and calculates what money is coming in, from where, and what money is being paid out, and to whom.

Marketing is the more creative side of the business. One task is research, which is carried out to find out what the customer wants. They are also responsible for advertising, for sales and for distribution. They have to direct the company to make products that the customers want, and they have to make the customers want to buy the products.

11. Writing a letter of complaint

(Musterlösung)
Dear Sir or Madam
Thank you for the delivery of our order on the 28th November. Unfortunately, I regret to inform you that the delivery has given me cause for complaint.
Instead of receiving twelve blue mini-stereos as we had ordered, we received six red mini-stereos and six blue mini-stereos. Three flat screens were missing, although we have been invoiced for them. 50 boxes of blank DVDs were delivered instead of the blank CDs we asked for, and finally, we received 200 black and white catalogues instead of ones in colour.
I suggest that the three missing flat screens and the six blue mini-stereos be delivered to us free of charge. Upon delivery, the red mini-stereos, which will be stored by us at our expense, can be collected. We will keep the 50 boxes of blank DVDs, providing that we receive a 15 % discount off the catalogue price. Please send the remaining 50 boxes of blank CDs to us within one week as they are urgently needed. We will dispose of the unusable catalogues.
Payment will follow only after all goods have been received.
Please provide confirmation that you agree with the above.
I hope that this incident does not spoil our business relations in any way.
Yours faithfully

12. Writing a quote

(Musterlösung)
Dear Sir or Madam
Thank you for your telephone call and your interest in our products. Following are the quotes for the items specified in your enquiry:

- 3000 postcards at € 0.18 each (but only when we are sent the final data and motifs).
- 1000 invitation cards at € 0.65 each (with orders of 750 cards and above, € 0.55 each).
- 4000 birthday cards at € 0.80 each.
- 1000 desk calendars with spiral binding at 1.75 € each.
- 100 yellow writing pads, A5, 50 pages each, at 1.39 € each.

As a first time customer we will offer you a 10% discount off the total order amount. The fourth time that you place an order with us with a value of above 10,000 € we will grant a bulk discount of 15%. Delivery ex works will take place within two weeks of receiving an order.
Payment terms are a 2% cash discount, if you pay within fourteen days, otherwise 30 days for the full invoice amount.
Thank you again for your interest. If you require any more information please do not hesitate to contact me.
Yours faithfully

13. Writing a reminder

(Musterlösung)
Dear Mr Miller
I am writing to you regarding your order number 1234/AD (shelves). Having looked at your account, it appears that you have not yet paid the invoice no. 8765 we sent you on the 30th August. This payment is now three months overdue.
We have already sent you two reminders, but have received no response to either of them, in the form of payment or otherwise. We regret that this is the case, as up until now we have had good business relations. We have done everything we can to resolve the matter, however "Jackson & Jonson" must now fulfil its obligations. To ensure an amicable end to the matter, we must insist that you send us either a cheque or pay by bank transfer within five days. Should this not happen, we will be obliged to begin legal proceedings. It seems clear to me that it is in the best interests of everyone involved to avoid this matter developing to such a stage. Allow me to express my hope that we can resolve the matter amicably. I await your response.
Yours sincerely

14. Preparing a presentation

(Musterlösung)
Good morning,
well, let me start be showing you last year's statistics
The graph shows the amount of employees who were off sick in the last year.
At the beginning of the year, in January and February, over 20 people were on sick leave at any one point In March that number rose to 35. However the next four months saw a steady decrease in the number of people on sick leave, reaching an annual low of 12 in July.
In August, there was a sudden increase in the number of people off sick. The number almost doubled, in comparison to July reaching 21 in August. This was followed by a drop back down to 12 in September.
Between September and October slightly more people had to take sick leave and the number rose to 18. In October and November, the number of people on sick leave remained steady, and there was a small increase in December to 19.
In conclusion, the main period is surprisingly the early part of the year, slumping in the summer, except for a sudden increase in August.

15. Writing a letter of application

(Musterlösung)
Dear Ms Brown
I recently saw your advertisement for an Assistant Office Manager on the internet, and would like to apply for the position.
In June 20.. I successfully completed my apprenticeship at Köpke & Sohn, a renowned German company, where I was employed as an Office Administrator. Now I am looking for a new challenge overseas. I want to work for an ambitious company which is growing quickly. Consequently, when I saw your advert I was certain that I had found a job which met all my requirements and one for which I was ideally suited.
Despite the fact that I am not a native English speaker, I have an excellent command of both spoken and written English. Following my aforementioned apprenticeship, I am also convinced that I could carry out all administrative duties admirably. In addition, tasks such as data entry pose no problems for me; I have an extremely good knowledge of Microsoft Office, as the attached certificate for a computer course shows. I also enclose my CV for your consideration.
I look forward to hearing from you.
Yours sincerely

MEDIATION

1. A memo

(Musterlösung)
To: Sales Department and all Heads of Departments
From: Managing Director
Subject: Meeting
The meeting regarding our poor quarterly sales figures will take place in room 101 (1st floor) on 15th July at 10am.
The meeting will last at least 4 hours excluding a 45-minute break.
Lunch will be provided.
Please remember to bring the attached figures.
If you are not able to take part in this important meeting, please let us know promptly.

2. An email

(Musterlösung)
Online-Outdooranbieter aus Newcastle (UK) ist an 200 2-Personenzelten, 300 4-Personenkuppelzelten, 200 Mumienschlafsäcken und 400 Luftmatratzen interessiert.
Will wissen ob

- Lieferung per LKW, Flugzeug oder Schiff
- Waren auf Lager oder produziert werden müssen
- Lieferung innerhalb von 2 Wochen möglich
- Mengenrabatt möglich? Möchte ein Rabatt von 20%.

Er erwartet unsere Bestätigung binnen 4 Stunden, da Waren dringend benötigt werden.

3. A good offer?

(Musterlösung)
Produktname: Canon MF-4150 schwarz-weiß Kopierer; **Multifunktionen:** Scanner, Drucker, Fax; **Auflösung:** 600 dpi; **Aufwärmzeit:** 5 Sekunden; **Kopierfarbe:** Schwarz-weiß; **Papierversorgung:** 300-Blätter Fach; **Papiergröße:** bis zu 216mm x 356mm; **Kopien pro Minute:** 21; **Automatischer Dokumenteneinzug:** ja, bis zu 35 Blätter; **Beidseitiger Druck:** ja; **Faxgeschwindigkeit:** 33600 bps; **Gewicht:** 12,8 kg; **Breite:** 40 cm; **Tiefe:** 42 cm; **Höhe:** 45 cm

4. Writing a summary

(Musterlösung)
Hello
I have just found an interesting advert. It is a fairly new agency, founded in 2004, with 15 employees. They claim to be a very innovative advertising agency and have developed into a well-known agency in the Rhine-Main area.
They are a start-up company, offering customized creative solutions of the highest standard for IT companies in several languages and are always looking for new challenges. Furthermore they claim to be unique. What do you think?
Maybe we could start a common campaign with them in order to save money.
Looking forward to your reply.
Kind regards

5. Taking messages

(Musterlösung)
Taking Messages Effectively
Understanding an English caller and passing on his message correctly is not that simple, particularly if the caller is a native speaker.
As a result, people often only understand parts of the important information. Make sure you get the following pieces of information. Here are some tips:
1. Names
Get both the first and last name (surname) and if necessary ask the caller to spell his name.
2. Company
Find out whether it is a business or a personal call, and whether your colleague knows the company.
3. Telephone number
Make sure you get the complete phone number, including the area code and country code if applicable. Repeat the number back to the caller to check that you have heard it correctly.

4. Reason for the call
Try to find out the reason the person is calling.
5. Action
Should the call be returned or is the message just for information? Will the caller ring again later?
6. Time of call
Make a note of when the call came in. This could be important for your colleague.

6. Chairing a meeting

(Musterlösung)
Besprechungsmanagement
Konferenzen können sehr produktiv sein. Sie können aber auch Zeitverschwendung sein.
Eine Konferenz sollte einen Zweck, eine Tagesordnung und einen Zeitrahmen haben. Sie sollten in der Lage sein, den Zweck der Konferenz in ein oder zwei Sätzen zu definieren. Erstellen Sie eine Tagesordnung. Setzen Sie ein Zeitlimit zu jedem Tagesordnungspunkt fest und benennen Sie die verantwortliche/vortragende Person. Setzen Sie einen Zeitrahmen. Legen Sie allermindestens einen Anfangs- und Endzeitpunkt fest.
Warten Sie nicht
Konferenzen müssen pünktlich beginnen. Warten Sie nicht auf das Eintreffen von Zuspätkommenden. Falls jemand zu spät kommt, gehen Sie nicht noch einmal zurück und wiederholen was schon gesagt wurde.
Bleiben Sie beim Thema
Jede Konferenz sollte einen „Themenbeobachter" haben. Seine Aufgabe ist es zu unterbrechen, wann immer die Diskussion vom diskutierten Thema abschweift.
Schreiben und versenden Sie Protokolle
Das Protokoll sollte festhalten, wer anwesend war, was diskutiert wurde, jegliche Übereinkünfte, die getroffen wurden und etwaige Umsetzungspunkte, die festgelegt (bestimmt) wurden.
Unverzüglich nach der Konferenz, in der Regel innerhalb von 24 Stunden, sollte das Protokoll der Konferenz verteilt werden.

7. A manual

(Musterlösung)
Placing and connecting the device
1. Pull out the rail as far as necessary and place the document shredder on the wastepaper basket. Make sure the document shredder is positioned in a way that it cannot fall down.
2. Slide the switch to the AUTO position and plug the plug into the socket.

Shredding paper
Caution: Remove paper clips because they may damage the appliance.
In the middle of the feeder is a sensor which switches on as soon as you insert paper. Therefore, insert smaller pieces of paper always in the middle of the feeder. You can shred up to 4 sheets of normal paper (of normal thickness, 70 g/m^2) at the same time. The appliance switches off automatically when the paper has gone through.
Paper jam?
If the paper is too thick, too many sheets of paper were inserted simultaneously or paper was inserted at an awkward angle, it might not be shredded correctly or a paper jam might occur. If a jam has occurred, slide the switch to REV (backwards) or FWD (forwards) respectively, to move the paper back and forth so that it can be removed.

8. Writing minutes

(Musterlösung)
Minutes
Monthly Sales Meeting: 22 September 20..
Present: Christian Altmann, Sandra Baker, Jonathan Beck, Steven Colee, David Grome, Inka Heynemeier, Fritz Leuermann, Robert Marston, Martin Runke, Stefanie Schmitt, Julius Strenke, Mike Swink, Karl Meier (Chairman).
Apologies: Susan Williams
Approval:
Minutes of meeting on 4th August are accepted unanimously.
Matters arising: None
Sales:
Sandra reports that UK sales have fallen by 4 per cent compared to June, which had also seen a drop of 3 per cent compared to March to May.
- Sandra to prepare a sales report of the last six months by 30th September.

Advertising budget:
Increase in advertising budget for next year is approved. Robert gives details of problems with "StarTime" advertising agency and recommends a change in strategy. It is agreed that a new advertising agency is needed.
- Steven to provide overview of advertising expenses by 7th October.
- Robert to visit "StarTime" agency on Friday, 26th September, to discuss campaign problems.

Sales Conference:
Hotel costs will be much higher than last year. The preferred conference room is not available in March or April.
- Inka to look into alternative locations and provide pricing information at next meeting.

Any other business:
Bert Watson, head of US sales, will be in the London office on 15th December.
Next meeting:
Monday, 13th October 20..

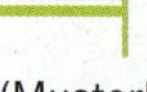

9. A German website

(Musterlösung)
Strategy Counts ist das führende Marketingunternehmen in London. Viele unserer Kunden kommen aus den Bereichen Finanzen und Versicherung. Strategy Counts verfügt über innovative Mittel zur Lokalisierung Ihrer Zielgruppe. Strategy Counts plant für Sie effektiv. Wir schaffen sichtbare Präsenz in den relevanten Medien und optimieren Ihren Geldeinsatz. In Großbritannien und nun auch in ganz Europa werden Sie von unserer Kompetenz profitieren.
Wir sind seit 1987 erfolgreich. Die Erfolgsformel hat sich von „Wer hat die besten Produkte oder die besten Dienstleistungen?" zu „Wer besitzt das beste Marketing?" verändert.
Gemäß diesem Motto steht Ihr Unternehmenserfolg immer in unserem Mittelpunkt. Unsere Referenzen und die vielen zufriedenen Kunden sprechen für sich selbst. Durch unser Streben nach hohen Qualitätsstandards und unsere Erfahrung besitzen wir die Fähigkeit, Sie auf professionelle und geeignete Art in diesem sensiblen und anspruchsvollen Marktsegment zu beraten.

10. Business visits

(Musterlösung)
Geschäftsbesuche in den USA

- Geschäftsbesuche starten extrem pünktlich, ein Zu-spät-Kommen wirft ein schlechtes Licht auf Sie. Deshalb pünktlich oder sogar zu früh erscheinen und bei Verspätungen Bescheid geben.
- Bei einem Treffen zum Essen beginnt das Meeting entweder gleich nach der Essensbestellung oder gleich nachdem alle Teilnehmer ihre Plätze genommen haben. Die private Unterhaltung findet im Gegensatz zu vielen anderen Ländern erst nach dem geschäftlichen Teil statt.
- In vielen amerikanischen Unternehmen gibt es Frauen in Führungspositionen, seien Sie also nicht überrascht, wenn Ihr Geschäftspartner eine Frau ist. Stellen Sie keine privaten Fragen und verabreden Sie sich nicht privat.
- Beim Geschäftstreffen stellt sich üblicherweise jeder mit festem Schütteln der rechten Hand vor.
- Visitenkarten werden in der Regel nicht automatisch ausgetauscht. Bitten Sie darum wenn Sie sie benötigen. Ihre eigene Karte können Sie anbieten.

11. Being successful

(Musterlösung)

The right tone for your business success

Professional success and good manners are directly related. If you express yourself and behave correctly you will not only score with your customers and business partners but also with your colleagues.
Here is a short extract on how to behave in style.

Greet while standing

Both men and women stand up to greet someone. The position they hold plays no role. Shake hands and remember to give a firm handshake. Look your partner in the eyes at the same time as shaking their hand. Introduce yourself with your first and last name (surname). If you have got a title, do not mention it. You may sound conceited if you emphasize it.

Lead the way

Lead the way, no matter if you're accompanying a customer from the company entrance to the conference room or a business partner from the workshop to the canteen. Your visitor doesn't know his way around.

Switch off your mobile phone

Under no circumstances should your private mobile ring in the office. Switch it off or mute it. Even vibration is inappropriate in meetings. If you really expect an important call, you should announce it in advance. Leave the room to take the call.

Keep things in order

Show professionalism in the way you prepare your documents. A pile of loose notes is taboo in meetings. A frantic search is time-consuming and gives an unstructured impression. Use folders or files to file your papers and materials tidily.

Dress correctly

Men: suits with extravagant patterns or flashy colours often have an irritating effect. A dark blue and charcoal grey suit always works. Men can use stronger colours for shirts and ties. But light-coloured socks are still frowned upon.

Ladies: simple and elegant is best. Do not drape yourself with too many necklaces and accessories. Sleeveless tops or tops with a plunging neckline are as improper as very short skirts. Women have a greater colour variety than their male colleagues, but beware of glaring vivid colours.

12. Holding presentations

(Musterlösung)

1. Wichtig: Publikum kennen und präsentiert, was sie benötigen. Bei der Präsentationserstellung ans Publikum denken. Stellt sicher, dass sie folgen werden. Bei Nichtgefallen kann man trotz guter Vorbereitung auf taube Ohren stoßen.
2. Unterlagen/Material gut kennen. Präsentation mit Freunden üben, vor Spiegel und mit anderen Kollegen. Bei Präsentation in Fremdsprache, Text vorher aufnehmen und einige Male anhören bevor man, falls möglich, mit einem Muttersprachler übt.
3. Vortragende ist Schauspieler. Sicherstellen, dass körperliche Erscheinung und ein gut gewählter Ton zum Anlass passen. Falls das Thema ernst ist, formell/ernst sein. Immer gut Präsentation mit Eisbrecher anzufangen.
4. Publikum ruhig und entspannt durch Materialien führen. Langsam und klar sprechen, sich jedem im Publikum zuwenden, selbst der am weitesten entfernten Person.

Deshalb folgenden Tipps während Präsentation folgen:

- Mit Überzeugung sprechen
- Glauben was man sagt und dadurch Zuhörer überzeugen
- Nicht ablesen. Notizen zu Hilfe zu nehmen ist okay aber nur kurz und oberflächlich
- Augenkontakt mit Publikum halten. Direkten Augenkontakt mit einzelnen vermittelt Gefühl, als wenn sie an der Präsentation teilnehmen.
- Handouts erstellen, nicht einfach nur eine PowerPoint Präsentation. Publikum mit Handouts der wichtigsten Informationen versorgen, so dass sie diese behalten können.
- Wissen, wann es aufzuhören gilt. Fall anbringen, aber nicht zu lange präsentieren sonst vergisst Publikum Gesagtes.

13. Translating for a website

(Musterlösung)
Travelfun products are manufactured to the highest quality standards. Throughout the manufacturing process, all items are subject to continuous inspection. In the unlikely event of a claim, the Travelfun warranty is applied as follows: The warranty covers material and workmanship-related defects only and is limited to the product's value. Defects due to improper handling/transport by third parties are not covered and cannot be accepted. In order to file a claim, presentation of proof of purchase (receipt) and filled-in guarantee card is mandatory. The 24-month warranty period begins on the date of purchase. In case of a valid claim, Travelfun has the right to exchange the item rather than repair it. Any claims beyond materials and quality cannot be accepted. In case of a valid claim of an item that is not available anymore or for which no more spares are available, Travelfun reserves the right to offer a comparable item in exchange. This warranty is supplementary to standard consumer laws.
As damage due to improper handling by third parties isn't covered by the warranty, here is some advice. After every trip examine all luggage immediately and as soon as you receive it from baggage reclaim (i.e. even before passing customs). In case any damage is found, you must immediately file a verbal and written claim with the respective handling agent at their helpdesk. Insist on written confirmation of the damaged incurred. Usually, if your claim is registered immediately, you can expect quick and generous action by the handling agent. In case you may require an expert's written opinion or quote, your friendly specialist retailer will only be too happy to help. Also for complete insurance coverage, buy additional luggage insurance.

14. Breaking into the European market

(Musterlösung)

General terms and conditions

1. **Right to exchange or return:** You have the unconditional right to return all goods bought at Largos free of charge within 14 days of delivery to Largos GmbH, without having to state your reasons.
2. **Delivery proviso:** Deliveries can be made whilst stocks last. We only deliver within Europe.
3. **Delivery costs:** At Largos you generally pay a flat rate of € 4.95 for delivery, regardless of the value of the order. This covers part of the packaging, delivery and postage costs. The rest is paid for you by Largos. In exceptional cases, we have to charge a higher flat rate. This will be specified accordingly.
   Should delivery be undertaken in several stages for technical or logistic reasons, we will of course only charge you once for delivery costs.
4. **Transfer of ownership:** Goods remain the property of Largos GmbH until payment has been received in full.
5. **Payment, due date, failure to pay:** Payment for goods is to be made by credit card or direct debit. Largos reserves the right to exclude certain modes of payment in individual cases.
   Unfortunately, we cannot accept payment sent in the form of cash or cheques. We exclude any liability for loss.

We will not charge your credit card until your goods leave our warehouse.
In the case of returns, the amount paid will be refunded.
Should your credit or debit card have insufficient credit, we reserve the right to invoice you for the costs incurred in making requests for payment.

15. The Autumn Fair

(Musterlösung)

Vorstellung:

- Die Autumn Fair/Herbstmesse ist die größte Messe in Großbritannien mit vielen Hauptmarken, europäischen Lieferanten und unabhängigen Designern, welche den Besuch lohnen
- Große Auswahl an Unternehmensaufbauseminaren, Trendvorschauen, Vorführungen und Ausstellungen

Angaben zur Messe:

- 2 Hauptbereiche - Geschenke und Wohnen - mit 2.000 Ausstellern in 9 Produktbereichen
- gute Einkaufsgelegenheit für Weihnachtsartikel und um eine Vorschau auf Markteinführungen des nächsten Jahres zu bekommen
- größte Herbsteinkaufsgelegenheit da dreimal so groß wie andere Messen
- über 500.000 Produkte
- 40.000 neue Markteinführungen
- über 2.000 Aussteller
- mehr als 60.000 Besucher aus aller Welt

Produktkategorien:

Kunst, Taschen, Geschenke, Kerzen, Mode, Produkte für Badezimmer, Innenausstattung, Modeaccessoires, Grußkarten, Schmuck, Spielzeug, Werbegeschenke

Genannte Ausstellungsgründe:

- beste Einkaufsgelegenheit der Saison
- die mehr als 60.000 Besucher sind kaufinteressiert
- der Ausstellungszeitpunkt ist bestens geeignet da Besucher Weihnachtsgroßeinkäufe tätigen und auf der Suche nach Frühlingsware sind
- Gelegenheit tausende von Einzelhändlern mit großer Einkaufsbereitschaft zu treffen
- Kontaktaufnahme zu unabhängigen, Internet-, oder auch Versandhändlern möglich
- Käufer aus ganz GB und tausende aus aller Welt
- Möglichkeit, von der globalen Marketingkampagne zu profitieren, die auf eine enorme Datenbank zielt

Nachfragen an Autumn Fair Sales; E-Mail: sales@autumnfair-wvd.com
Öffnungszeiten
Samstag, 6. September
10.00 - 17.00 Uhr
Sonntag, 7. September - Mittwoch, 10. September
09.00 - 18.00 Uhr

INTERAKTION

Individuelle Lösungen

mock exams

Prüfung 1 Stufe I (A2, Waystage)

Rezeption
Hörverständnis

AB-Nachricht für: Thomas Scott
Abwesend von: 20. **bis:** 23. April
Wünscht Weiterleiten der Gespräche: nein
Alternativ erreichbar unter: 0176 32458741 (Handynr.)
Weitergabe der Alternativnummer an Anrufer: nur an bestimmte
Erwartet wichtige Anrufe von: Tony Smith von KT Limited, Sam Finch von YTS and Dave Hammond von Target.

Rezeption
Leseverständnis
(in Stichworten)

1. Sie sind von der Menge der E-Mails gestresst/sie wollen verhindern, dass die Absender eine schnelle Antwort erwarten/ sie wollen erst mal sehen, wer am Telefon ist. (Sie sind für kürzere oder längere Zeit nicht im Büro anwesend.)
2. es dürfen keine internen E-Mails in der Firma versendet werden
3. miteinander sprechen von Angesicht zu Angesicht; zu telefonieren
4. 37
5. Sie überprüfen, ob neue Mails angekommen sind

Produktion
(Musterlösung)

Betreff: Out of office
Dear Sir or Madam
Thank you for your message.
I am on a business trip in Holland at the moment and will be back in the office on Monday, 26th April. I will reply to your email as soon as possible when I return.
In the meantime, if your message concerns an urgent delivery, please contact my assistant, Kirsten Müller, on +49 (0)161 883 672 323 or at k.mueller@traber-wvd.com.
General product enquiries should be sent to Loreley Gibson at l.gibson@traber-wvd.com.
Best regards

Mediation
(in Stichworten)

Wie man Abwesenheitsnachrichten verfasst

Stil: formellen Ton anwenden. Mit neutraler und formeller Begrüßung wie „Sehr geehrte Damen und Herren“ anfangen. Niemals in E-Mails und Briefen „Meine Damen und Herren“ benutzen, das ist nur für formelle Reden.
Höflichkeit: dem Absender danken. „Danke für die Nachricht“ ist freundlicher als nur „Danke“.

Wichtige Details: Abwesenheitsgrund nur angeben falls er relevant ist. Genau angeben wann man zurück ist unter Angabe des genauen Datums mit Wochentag zur Vermeidung von Missverständnissen.
Positive Angaben: Sagen was man machen wird und nicht was man nicht machen wird. Schreiben Sie „Ich werde Ihre E-Mail beantworten sobald ich es nach meiner Rückkehr einrichten kann". Mitteilen, ob die E-Mail weitergeleitet wurde.
Alternativen: Genaue Angabe von Kontaktpersonen (Namen, Position, E-Mail Adressen und Telefonnummer mit Landesvorwahl), die während Ihrer Abwesenheit dringende Nachrichten bearbeiten.
Unterschrift: Unterschrift mit vollständigem Namen des Unternehmens anfügen falls jemand etwas per Post schicken möchte.

Mündliche Prüfung
individuelle Lösung

Prüfung 2 Stufe II (B1, Threshold)

Rezeption
Hörverständnis
Kunde (Firma und Name): Duggins Ltd. (Bournemouth), David Duggins
Bestellnummer: DG 4829
Referenznummer: GB0253
Problem mit Bestellung: beschädigte Ware
Details: Kisten von außen beschädigt; Spediteur ließ einige Kisten während des Entladens fallen;
Problembehandlung: Ersatzwaren losschicken und beschädigte Ware abholen

Rezeption
Leseverständnis
(in Stichworten)

1. Probleme, Fehler, Pech/Unglück mit Produkten oder Dienstleistungen
2. Viele Unternehmen versuchen, Beschwerden zu ignorieren oder sie als nicht relevant abzutun. Besser: mit Beschwerden umgehen und sie als Vorteil nutzen
3. Sie geben Zeit, sich mit dem Problem zu beschäftigen, es zu lösen und dem Kunden zu antworten

Art der Beschwerde: Briefe; **Häufigkeit:** sehr häufig;
Voraussetzung: wenn eine Adresse vorhanden ist
Art der Beschwerde: direkte Ansprache an den Verkäufer;
Häufigkeit: häufigste Form; **Voraussetzung:** direkter Kundenkontakt
Art der Beschwerde: Telefongespräche; **Häufigkeit:** häufig
Voraussetzung: Telefon wird für Kundenkontakt benutzt – Nummern bekannt;
Art der Beschwerde: E-Mail; **Häufigkeit:** /
Voraussetzung: E-Mailadressen für Kunden zugänglich

Mediation
(Musterlösung)

- letzte Lieferung hat schon wieder Anlass zur Beschwerde gegeben.
- 3 von 10 Kisten waren stark beschädigt; wurden beim Ausladen vom Spediteur fallen gelassen
- Hälfte der Lampen und Lampenfassungen waren zerbrochen und ist somit unverkäuflich
- Schon das 2. Mal in Folge und etliche Lampen waren reserviert für wichtige Kunden und bis zum Ende der Woche versprochen
- Verlust von einigen treuen Kunden vermutet
- Zur Vermeidung bestehen Duggins Ltd. auf sofortige und kostenlose Lieferung von 30 Lampen Nr. K3P754 durch einen anderen Spediteur
- Wenn Bedingungen nicht erfüllt werden, werden Duggins Ltd. um Entschädigung bitten, um Verluste zu decken

Produktion
(Musterlösung)
Ref: order no. DG 4829
Dear Ms. Jenkins
I regret to inform you that a customer contacted us this morning with a complaint about damaged goods (see order number above). This is not the first time that customers have contacted us about deliveries that have been made by your company.
We are certain that the goods left our company in good condition and as a result, we conclude that the damage must have occurred during delivery.
Up to now we have had a good working relationship and I hope that there won't be any more problems in future.
Please can you confirm that you will deliver a replacement delivery to the client within the next two days. I very much hope that this further delivery will be carried out to our complete satisfaction.
Yours sincerely

Mündliche Prüfung
individuelle Lösung

Prüfung 3 Stufe III (B3, Vantage)

Rezeption
Hörverständnis
(in Stichworten)

1. Toys Direct B.V.
2. travelled by ferry (from Gothenburg) and train (from Kiel)/ journey time: about 15 hours
3. They're the leading toy manufacturer in Sweden and throughout Scandinavia, but they don't really have a presence on the German market. They are looking for partners in Germany who would be prepared to introduce their products onto the German market, selling them under license from them.
4. It's over 150 years old.
5. 2,500 employees; 1,750 in Mölndal, just outside Gothenburg and 750 in Karlstad
6. From 10-2 (with an hour lunch break at 12).
7. They're staying in Hamburg today and tomorrow they're in Berlin for two days.

Rezeption
Leseverständnis
(in Stichworten)

1. Is based on the idea that the individual is both willing and able to do a good job. A Swedish manager is a coach and often delegates tasks and authority. Employees of all levels have the freedom to make decisions and solve unexpected problems without asking superiors for permission. A good manager leads through cooperation and agreement, plus they are good at listening and rational rather than emotional.
2. It relates to how people feel in terms of controlling and being controlled within a hierarchical situation. In Sweden the power distance is very small and a lot smaller than in most countries.
3. Personal status is of little importance. No-one seen as being socially superior. Managers don't give signs of their status and employees don't feel inferior. Use of first names at work.
4. Problem-solving is informal and pragmatic. It can mean bypassing one or more layers of executives.

5. In most countries, seniority plays a part in promotion. In Sweden, however, actual work performance tends to be of greater importance.
6. Being late and not being direct (preferring to make small-talk over talking business).

Produktion
(Musterlösung)
Dear Sir or Madam
We saw your website on the Internet and understand that you are a producer of high-tech products such as personal computers, notebooks, printers, monitors, cameras, etc.
We are a large producer of high-quality microchips and circuit boards and one of the leading manufacturers in the supply industry. We offer state-of-the-art solutions for which we are well-known. Our products are reliable and long lasting.
We already have customers in Germany, France, Italy and Spain and we are planning to enter the Swedish market this year. Therefore we are looking for Swedish customers who require top-quality manufacturing made in Europe. That is why we believe you are the right company and would like to enter into business relations with you.
The enclosed catalogue will give you further information on our company and products.
We would be happy to negotiate prices, payment and delivery terms of delivery and payment with you in person during a meeting in Munich.
We look forward to hearing from you soon.
Yours faithfully

Mediation
(Musterlösung)
PRODATA B.V.:
- technology company that operates in more than 170 countries around the world
- explore how technology and services can help people and companies address their problems and challenges, and realize their potential, aspirations and dreams
- apply new thinking and ideas to create more simple, valuable and trusted experiences with technology, continuously improving the way customers live and work
- offer a complete technology product portfolio
- provide infrastructure and business offerings
- offer consumers a wide range of products and services from digital photography to digital entertainment and from computing to home printing
- offer right products, services and solutions to customers' specific needs

Fast Facts
- founded in 1975
- Corporate headquarters in Stockholm (Sweden)
- CEO is Kalle Bergstrom
- among the world's largest IT companies, with a turnover of 104.3 billion € in 2007

Contribution
- want to make an economic, intellectual and social contribution to each country and community in which they do business
- key areas of contribution are reducing electronic waste, raising standards in global supply chain and increasing access to information technology

Mündliche Prüfung
individuelle Lösung